Step Up America!

A CASE FOR A NATIONAL SERVICE PROGRAM

Ted Hollander

outskirts press

Table of Contents

The reader should note that the term "national service" is used in the book where national service is presented in general terms as a concept, and "National Service" (with the first letters capitalized) is used to specifically identify the program the author is recommending.

Introduction

Are you concerned that your country threatens to renege on the traditional "contracts" made with the rest of the world to protect the planet and its resources? Does it trouble you that we no longer extend a welcoming hand to political refugees and economic migrants, and that we no longer wish to trade freely with our neighbors and partners?

Do you believe that our wars over the past six decades have been ill conceived and poorly managed, and that our electorate is insufficiently educated and enlightened to sustain "government by the people"?

If you are dissatisfied as I am by the current state of affairs, and think new solutions are needed, then read on as I make my case for National Service as a powerful force for transformation and rededication.

What do I mean by National Service? Its central component is the requirement of virtually everyone coming of age in the United States to serve a mandatory period of time doing some form of service in the national interest, giving back something in return for the opportunities and rewards that many of us are so fortunate to enjoy. The outcome, I believe, will be an enlightened youth more capable of getting our nation back on track and moving forward.

Our program could offer several paths toward filling the requirement, some under the umbrella of National Service, others perhaps in lieu of the program but contributory to the national good in some other way. Military service is the most obvious form of participation and will be chosen by many. Other elements of the program would include a variety of civilian community service assignments both here and abroad, as listed in Chapter Two. Civilian service might include a commitment to some of the existing service organizations such as the Peace Corps and AmeriCorps VISTA.

Along with a sense of accomplishment and learning one or more skills, every participant would get a broader exposure to other ways of life and to other segments of society. These benefits, along with a unique education in life skills and civic participation, will produce an enlightened youth, and over time an entire enlightened populace, which will help America regain its preeminent leadership position. We can then step forward with confidence to meet the challenges of the future.

I served a two-year tour plus a short extension in the Marine Corps during the interlude after the Korean War and before the Vietnam conflict had heated up. After my somewhat sheltered childhood, being an enlisted man turned out to be a very positive maturing experience; it has significantly influenced my thinking and has provided some of the background to the issues and situations that I will cover in the following chapters. For example, I lament the fact that I did this tour *after* rather than *before* college. Had conscription of 18-year-olds in my proposed National Service program been mandatory at that time, I would have been in a better frame of mind to take advantage of my college education when I got there.

I like to think of myself politically as essentially a centrist. However, some of the recommendations I will make in the following chapters are very progressive. Then again, you will also find more than a hint of social conservatism in some of my other positions. This is fine. In spite of the fierce partisan wrangling that goes on in Washington DC, the issues and actions facing this country are not at all black and white. No one can refute the fact that much of what we are now doing, or planning to do, in the way of policy formation is drawing us deeper and deeper into the abyss of mediocrity, inequality, and failure. While we need to stand by our basic values, we also need to give some real "power" to the people by educating them to stand up to their elected officials and to hold them accountable for their actions.

When I started writing the first edition of this book in 2014, I thought the nation was on a downward spiral. Then as we moved through President Obama's last year in office and into President Trump's first year I realized that we had completely lost our way. Looking back to 2013, consider how Congress dealt with Section 4 of the 14th Amendment which confirms the validity of public debt. Congress completely ignored Section 4 rather than work out a political compromise that would keep the government running. Consider as well how the nation's most classified surveillance programs were entrusted to Edward Snowden, an inadequately vetted individual who was the subject of investigation for NSA job-related improprieties. Look at how we were caught red-handed eavesdropping on the cell phone communications of Angela Merkel, the head of state of one of our closest allies. And how humiliating is it that our government launched the most important social program since Medicare without verifying that www.health.gov, the $300MM website that was to enable the public to learn about their choices and to sign up, actually functioned.

Such poor preparation is sadly still with us under the new Trump administration. One of its first actions was to place a ban on persons entering the U.S. from seven Muslim countries without having first consulted most of its team to understand the political ramifications of such an order or preparing any of its agencies to execute the ruling. In a matter of a few hours the U.S. made a mockery of America's reputation as a welcoming melting pot for all. In another embarrassment the new president named as his National Security Advisor Michael Flynn, a general known for his "Flynn facts" habit of falsifying information, only to dismiss him three weeks later for falsely representing his discussions with the Russian ambassador about issues related to national security. And on it goes as the Trump administration thoughtlessly damages our good relations with our neighbor and trading partner Mexico, our long-term ally Australia, our NATO partners, and the minorities and religious and ethnic groups that we have insulted here and abroad. As I write this I am hopeful that the country will pull itself together and will support the new president when appropriate, constructively criticize or strongly oppose him when necessary, and participate in our government to the maximum extent of our individual capabilities.

What can be done to get us back on track? I will say now, and repeat it as we go along, that I am not talking about making America "great again". Even with our shortcomings, we remain the shining example of democratic government and de facto leader of the free world. Rather, I am talking about meeting the challenges that I will describe as we go forward, correcting our mistakes, and making us greater. The people are willing, in fact anxious, to meet the challenges, if they have the tools. It is the government that is dysfunctional; it is the government that must change its culture if it has any hope of meeting these challenges. Why do I think a universal National Service program is the answer? I firmly believe that such a program can turn our youth into a powerful force for positive action. Through National Service they can gain a better understanding of the issues facing us, and how to work with the rest of the world to solve them. This subject has been addressed off and on by several outspoken advocates to whose voices I now add mine. During the 2016 primary debates, former Maryland

Governor Martin O'Malley made a plea for national service. So have journalist David Brooks in his *New York Times* columns and James Stone in his powerful *5 Easy Theses — Common Solutions to America's Greatest Economic Challenges.* Hillary Clinton in the final months of her campaign came out with a very comprehensive national program with a goal of enlisting and training five million volunteers ages 18 to 30 in community and national service. William F. Buckley back in 1990 made an impassioned plea for national service in his book, *Gratitude,* Reflections on What We Owe to our Country, about which you will hear more later.

Also in my book you will hear from General Stanley McChrystal, our leading proponent of national service . In addition several colleges are currently addressing national service in a variety of ways. Tufts University implemented a pilot program in 2015 offering to fund a bridge year between high school graduation and the start of the freshman year to selected students who enroll in a program sponsored by a recognized non-profit public service organization. Tulane University coordinates with AmeriCorps VISTA in providing paid fellowships for selected students to participate in public service in New Orleans.[1] Burnout from AP courses, sports, and a myriad of extracurricular activities in middle and high school are contributing to an increased interest in a gap year. According to the Department of Education, the average student entering college right after high school takes six, not four, years to complete, whereas those who take a gap year are more likely to complete their college requirements in four. The down side of spending gap years at such private programs as the National Outdoor Leadership School in Wyoming is the financial cost. Then too, there are volunteer opportunities with AmeriCorps and other organizations that combine hard work with a modest stipend and money toward college later. Some of the universities, Boston College and the University of North Carolina for example, actually offer some additional financial aid for those taking a gap year. In return, they enroll a more mature and focused student.[2] National Service, however, will be for everyone and it will ensure that all high school graduates have had the benefit of a "gap" period before entering college or embarking on a career path.

Chapter One
Why a National Service program?

Ask not what your country can do for you. Ask what you can do for your country.

John F. Kennedy Inaugural Address January 20, 1961

President Kennedy had it right: we need to recommit our nation and its citizens to a greater sense of public duty if we are to end the downward spiral on which the U.S. is currently bound. Since the end of World War II, we as a people have become increasingly conflicted, wanting more entitlements from our country yet giving less. It has become painfully clear that, for every step forward, we take two steps back, socially, economically, and morally. The marginal responses of which our federal government seems capable will no longer suffice. We need truly revolutionary thinking and action that take us well beyond the social and economic benefits gained by the post-industrial and digital revolutions. We see bits and pieces, here and there, of revolution against the establishment, for example in the movements espoused by Occupy Wall Street and Black Lives Matter. We see it also in the clamor for a federally-mandated $15 minimum wage, and the campaign promises of 2016 presidential candidate Bernie Sanders for universal health care, free college education, an end to poverty and elimination of fossil fuels.

Lacking sufficient support from the top down as well as from the bottom up, these efforts remain only "bits and pieces". In May 2016 consumer advocate Ralph Nader held a 4-day conference, "Breaking Through Power" in Washington DC. The conference marked the 50th anniversary of Nader's seminal book *Unsafe at any Speed* which exposed the designed-in dangers of America's automobiles. The book had been an instant bestseller, bringing much-needed attention to the failings of the entire automotive industry and prompted Congress to pass the National Traffic and Motor Vehicle Safety Act of 1966, mandating seat belts and leading to a host of other automotive safety features. Nader's 2016 conference, sponsored by his Center for Study of Responsive Law, featured speakers presenting innovative ideas and strategies designed to strengthen our civic culture, make existing civic groups more effective, and make corporations more accountable to stakeholders. If Nader, his "Raiders", and other independent groups of educated enlightened civic-minded people can produce such transformative changes without direct government support, consider what could be done if we could implement a National Service program for the millions of young people who come of age each year. I ask you to imagine a complete culture change, one initially forced upon us perhaps, but eventually embraced by all. I am speaking of reconstituting a sense of national mission — call it mindful patriotism, if you will. Anything less will not be good enough to restore our national vigor and influence.

The idea of national service is nothing new or radical. It goes all the way back to the eighth and ninth centuries AD when Charlemagne, the great military leader and unifier of crown and church in most of the nations of Europe, required military service of all land owners and promoted civic service as a foundation of the community.[3]

Tom Friedman and Michael Mandelbaum in their book *That Used to be Us* claim that the country "has strayed from three of the core values on which American greatness depended in the past."[4] The first departure they cite is the shift from long-term investment to short-term gratification, in which we postpone important actions and delay needed reforms in order to reap profits today. The second is the loss of confidence in our institutions and their leaders. But it is the third departure that I wish to emphasize here: "a weakening of our sense of shared national purpose, which propelled us in — and was reinforced by — the struggle against fascism in World War II and against communism in the Cold War."[4] The Cold War, in the authors' opinions did, despite all its dangers, bring one benefit: "It fostered a feeling of American solidarity, a shared sense of the national interest, as well as a seriousness about governance, which could rally the country to do important and constructive things at home and abroad."[4] It is this very need for sharing that the National Service program addresses.

Much has been written disparagingly about national service in the past. Some would deny the broad social benefits of a program like this; others argue that it simply will not work. I obviously disagree on both counts. To make my case I will not only provide successful examples of such programs as they have been used in the past, but I will also provide a broader definition of public service, one that will have relevance to the many talents and interests of our diverse population while meeting a wider array of social needs. Do not regard the details that I offer as gospel, but think in terms of possibilities. Better yet, think of how we can make the concept work. For starters, let's agree that "we the people" currently fall far short of pulling together in the national interest.

Tim Shriver, the Chairman of the Special Olympics, thinks leadership has failed to reach out to our better selves. He writes, "It is sad to see how difficult it is for politicians today to ask people to do anything other than enhance their well-being. I still see this enormous hunger for public purpose — people wanting to be part of something bigger than themselves, people volunteering to help others, looking for ways to join in solving big problems. But our political leaders won't channel all this good will into national purpose and I don't understand why."[5]

Friedman and Mandelbaum have addressed this failure, describing what happened after the terrorist attack on the World Trade Center and the Pentagon in 2001. They noted that the whole country was ready to answer the call when President Bush vowed to go after the terrorists, but that was as far as he went. "He never rallied Americans to even the most simple, necessary, and obvious collective action — to free ourselves from our bondage to imported oil, for example, by using less gasoline and paying more for it through a gasoline 'Patriot Tax.'"[5] The authors went on to quote Harvard political philosopher Michael J. Sandel, who said that the armed forces have become "the last repository of civic idealism and sacrifice for the sake of the common good. We have outsourced and confined to the military a concentrated expression of the civic ideals and patriotism that should be shared by all American citizens."[5]

"We have also outsourced sacrifice. If World War II was 'the good war,' and the Korean War 'the forgotten war,' and Vietnam 'the controversial war,' the conflict that began with the attacks of September 11, 2001, and has sent U.S. troops to Afghanistan and Iraq for more than a decade can be called 'the 1 percent war.' The troops deployed to these combat zones and their immediate families make up less than 1 percent of the population of the United States. The rest of us contribute nothing. We won't even increase our taxes, even through a surcharge on gasoline, to pay for these wars. So we end up asking 1 percent of the country to make the ultimate sacrifice and the other 99 percent to make no sacrifice at all."[5]

New York Times columnist Bob Herbert concurs: "The Idea that the United States is at war and hardly any of its citizens are paying attention to the terrible burden being shouldered by its men and women in uniform is beyond appalling."[6] Herbert notes that we seem to have plenty of time to give to Lady Gaga, Tea Party crackpots, fantasy football, and our "obsessively narcissistic tweets," but when it comes to caring about American soldiers fighting and dying in a foreign land, the same public is singularly uninterested. He continues, "I would bring back the draft in a heartbeat. Then you wouldn't have these wars that last a lifetime", and you wouldn't have 29 year old soldiers like Sgt. First Class Lance Vogeler killed while serving a 12th tour…yes, that's right, his 12th — four in Iraq and eight in Afghanistan….We simply don't have enough volunteers to fight these endless wars."[6] Summarizing, Mr. Herbert states that "the wars in Afghanistan and Iraq have been world-class fiascos. To continue them without taking serious account of the horrors being endured by our troops and their families is just wrong."[6]

One way to take "serious account" of this terrible inequity would be to restore the draft so that practically all families will in the future be affected. The war in Afghanistan, having lasted 15 years, is the longest in our history. After all this time and all the bloodshed and lives lost, most of us would be hard-pressed to say what we are still doing there. The Afghan army, try as it may to adopt the techniques of modern warfare and troop discipline, still cannot function effectively without substantial support from the U.S. and NATO forces. Add to this the fact that the Afghan civilian government, our supposed ally, is rife with corruption and political infighting, and lacks a cohesive vision for the future. Pakistan, which we once thought would cooperate with us in stabilizing Afghanistan, not only cannot be trusted to do as it says in return for massive infusions of development money, but it tolerates clandestine operations that specifically aim at sabotaging progress within its neighbor's borders. To those who still question

President Obama's decision to wind down and finally end this war, I ask how can our society — both U.S. voters and our elected officials — continue to justify risking the lives of young men and women in the bubbling stewpot that is Afghanistan?

Paying Our Way

As of now, most estimates of the costs of the Iraq and Afghanistan wars are in the order of $2 trillion, and some experts conjecture that, before final accounting some years from now, this figure will grow to $4 trillion or even $6 trillion.

Paying for these wars is a particularly intractable problem. We are currently embroiled in a fierce ideological battle over how to have our cake and eat it too. The political Right's position, as previously represented by John Boehner's statements at the time of the 2013 Budget Sequestration, is that any discussion of increasing federal revenues — whether from additional taxes or through tax reform — to pay for any of the debts already incurred — is off the table. The Republican majority claims that higher taxes only hurt growth and discourage entrepreneurship, while preserving "entitlements" and other social programs that go to dropouts and other undeservings. The Left, led by current or former Democratic leaders like Barack Obama, Harry Reid, Hillary Clinton, Nancy Pelosi, and Charles Schumer, look for additional revenues through raising tax rates on the wealthy, closing corporate loopholes, and increasing job opportunities through stimulus programs and other expansions of the welfare state (typified by FDR's New Deal, LBJ's Great Society, and Obama's Affordable Healthcare).

Nowhere in all these debates is an answer to the question: Who will pay for our wars? Oh, let's not worry about that. We'll just keep the wars off the books. Then no one will pay, except perhaps our children and grand-children — and they won't know the difference, as it will all be mixed in with the rest of the huge mountain of debt we bequeath to them.

R. Russell Rumbaugh, former defense analyst on the Senate Budget Committee covering Defense and International Affairs and a highly respected authority on international security, in his *New York Times* article, "A Tax to Pay for the War" makes a good case for a war tax. On the brighter side, he states, "Military spending has been declining since 2009....At our current level of $646 billion, we are spending roughly 4 percent of GDP on national defense, well below Cold War averages."[7] The as yet unanswered question, Rumbaugh notes, is whether we can afford to pay more for national defense now, or do we continue to borrow, driving the national debt still further up? War spending — like all other forms of private and public spending — disrupts financial stability only when expenses exceed income. Four years ago, "the Senate Budget Committee adopted a bipartisan amendment requiring that wars be paid for. The Simpson-Bowles deficit reduction commission...proposed doing much the same thing."[7]

Rumbaugh goes on to state that "war traditionally has motivated major changes in tax policy. The Civil War brought the first [and temporary] income tax. World War I made the federal income tax permanent. World War II brought tax withholding. In 1969, at the height of the Vietnam War, the United States ran a budget surplus because of a tax surcharge Congress forced President Lyndon B. Johnson to accept."[7] We don't have anything similar in place now, but as Rumbaugh points out, it would be easy to implement a surcharge. "Since the Budget Control Act already caps military spending...any spending over the caps would require it. If we felt the need to use the military and could do so under the spending caps, as the Obama administration did in 2011 responding to the earthquake in Japan and the uprising in Libya, no surcharge would be necessary. But if military action required supplemental financing, any amount over the caps would be offset with new revenues raised by an automatic surcharge on taxes."[7]

"By tying military action to additional revenue, the president would actually have a freer hand in deciding when to use force. Every argument the Obama administration makes for military action would explicitly include a call for increased taxes, forcing the question of whether the stakes in the military situation are worth the cost."[7]

Rumbaugh closed his argument saying that "if military action is worth our troops' blood, it should be worth our treasure, too — not just in the abstract, but in the form of a specific ante by every American."[7]

Now of course, if President Trump realizes the huge increase in military spending that he proposes, attention to the problem becomes even more critical.

Regarding the tax portion, it is interesting to note that during election years politicians on both sides of the aisle, albeit more of them on the Right than the Left, lament our high taxes which they claim stifle business, reduce our ability to compete abroad, smother the middle class, and keep the underclass mired in place. The public, who have little to go on other than what their leaders tell them, too often believe what they hear.

And, while we're at it, let's talk about who is paying their fair share and who is not. The rich claim they're paying *more* than their fair share. Others contend that the rich enjoy unwarranted exclusions and deductions not available to the rest. This is an absurd argument. First of all "fair" is not a term that, from a practical standpoint, should be used at all in considering how much tax anyone should pay. The only way to be truly "fair" would be for all of us to pay the exact same amount, although one could also make a case that paying the same rate would be fair. As soon as we start working with a graduated rate, literal "fairness" goes out the window. Yet the U.S. could not function without a graduated rate. Therefore, instead of harping on a "fair share", we should be addressing an "efficient share", "economical share", "functional share" or something else more realistic. In actuality "a large majority of American households — about two out of three — pay less than 15 percent of income to the federal government through either income taxes or payroll taxes."[8] From this perspective, it can certainly be argued that this is a modest price to pay for what we get: military defense of our freedom; access to government subsidized health care; a safety net for the underprivileged; construction and maintenance of interstate highways, railways, airports, dams and waterways; federal assistance to education, and a variety of costly global aid initiatives. Further, almost half of our population pay no federal income tax at all because of the many deductions for which they are eligible. "This disconnect between what we pay and what we think we pay," writes *New York Times* journalist David Leonhardt, "is nothing less than one of the country's biggest economic problems."[8]

U.S. tax rates today are substantially lower than in past years. The maximum marginal tax rate in 1945, for example, was 94 percent, and during the Korean War it was 92 percent. By 2013 it had come down to a maximum of 39.6 percent for the top income bracket. Absent significant increases in the near future, our tax revenues will not keep pace with the escalating costs of our three largest entitlements, Medicare, Medicaid, and Social Security, not to mention pay for all the other items in the national budget. Although we have the largest military budget in the world, virtually all of the "rich" European countries, as well as Australia, New Zealand and Canada, rely on substantially higher personal income tax rates to fund their budgets. France, the *most* expensive, imposes personal taxes of 54 percent annually; Belgium, Italy, and Denmark are close behind.

Then too, let's examine the free handouts our federal government distributes in varying combinations to everyone, the Child Tax Credit, the reduced taxes applied to dividends and capital gains, the deductions for taxes paid to jurisdictions other than the federal government, deductions for charitable contributions, for certain medical expenses and home mortgages, etc., etc. Those of us on Medicaid or Medicare have our health care insurance subsidized by the federal government. Then for the poor and disadvantaged there are the Earned Income Tax Credit, food stamps and other welfare benefits.[9] But personal taxes are just one way to measure how citizens contribute to their country. Here's where a National Service program can change virtually every person's relationship to his or her community while having a profound impact on his or her own life.

The reader may question my patriotism and love for this country as he or she follows my sometimes harsh criticism of this great nation, but read on. I criticize the government, not the nation. Of course, criticism of the government is, I suppose, a criticism of all of us. We elected them. At any rate, one has to define the problem before presenting a solution. While I am committed to this cause, I also draw on others who are as passionate as I in their concerns.

Skin in the Game

We've all heard it. We all think it. If only our Congressman's son or daughter were required to do military service, our leaders would surely hesitate longer before entering some of our more questionable wars. A cliché? No! Anyone who has visited Walter Reed National Military Medical Center in Bethesda, Maryland would be inclined to exhaust all reasonable alternatives before exposing their children to the horrors of war. At Walter Reed, they would meet hundreds of amputees and other grievously wounded warriors returned from Iraq and Afghanistan, all of them trying against terrible odds to restore some semblance of their pre-war lives.

The fact is that our more privileged and well-connected young men and women do not go to war now in large numbers. That's because we have shifted responsibility for maintaining the security of the United States, and of our individual lives, to a very small number of fellow Americans. These days our protectors are largely ambitious youth looking for adventure, committed youth looking to do the right thing, immigrants hoping to expedite naturalization and citizenship status, and unemployed youth looking for a steady job.

To be historically accurate, it's not just our recent wars that have had this imbalance. Many of our past wars have been fought by a relative few as the more privileged bought their way out — either directly in the old days through hiring a conscript, or through influence that gives them exclusion. It wasn't right then, and it certainly isn't right now.

As Tom Brokaw wrote in his *New York Times* essay "The Wars That America Forgot About'" back in October 2010, the United States was then "in its ninth year of fighting in Afghanistan and Iraq, the longest wars in American history. Almost 5,000 men and women have been killed. More than 30,000 have been wounded, some so gravely they're returning home to become, effectively, wards of their families and communities."[10] Brokaw calculated that during those first nine years we spent more than $1 trillion on the war effort and related foreign aid, reconstruction, embassies, veterans' rehabilitation and health care and so on. We can expect to spend hundreds of billions of additional dollars as we finally withdraw. Yet you would not think this was an issue, based on the content of political campaigns and debates during those years.

In every instance the focus of candidates and of voters was on health care, taxes, jobs, marriage and gender equality, the deficit... hardly anything on "our" wars! Why? Because for the vast majority of Americans, unless they are enlisted in the armed services or have a family member serving, their economic well-being is their priority. According to Brokaw, "The all-volunteer uniformed services now represent less than 1 percent of the American population, but they're carrying 100 percent of the battle."[10]

If our recent elections had truly been about taking the country in a new direction, as the candidates all claimed, why weren't any of the candidates speaking up for sacrifice shared by all? Brokaw concludes, "No decision is more important than committing a nation to war. It is, as politicians like to say, about our blood and treasure. Surely blood and treasure are worthy of more attention than they've been getting."[10]

Well...this will change if the nation implements a mandatory national service requirement. Even those participants who choose to serve in one of the civilian service components will undergo an initial military training phase, enough to realize that it is unjust and inexcusable for the 1 percent to carry the full burden, and that service to country is truly a shared responsibility. And the political candidates who get elected to represent this new group will speak to those issues, too, because it will be something their constituents know and care about, personally.

General Stanley McChrystal, the former commander of international forces in Afghanistan, has also weighed in about the inequities inherent in our current volunteer army. Speaking at the annual Aspen Ideas Festival in June 2012, he said "I think if a nation goes to war, every town, every city needs to be at risk. You make that decision and everybody has skin in the game."[11]

Plenty of thoughtful people on the Left and Right agree. For one thing, mandatory participation in some form of national service brings together groups of people who might never have anything to do with one another under other circumstances, and it forces them to develop bonds of understanding and trust. This diversity will increase tolerance and openness, and studies have shown this can foster creativity and enhance performance.[12] And if national service encompasses a number of options beyond military service, other practical benefits follow.

Martin A. Dyckman, a respected political biographer, has written in favor of a national service program, comparing it to the Depression-era Civilian Conservation Corps that provided so many needed employment opportunities in the repair of roads and other infrastructure nationwide. He also implied that the fresh thinking generated by the experience of national service could have immense social benefits when these young people re-enter civilian life.[13] Of course, putting national service candidates to work on public infrastructure and other kinds of civilian jobs is bound to get pushback from private sector unions, conflicts that will have to be fairly resolved if the program is to succeed. Regardless of the final domestic civilian service mix, there are many benefits that will accrue if we also add an international aid element, for it will show us once again to be a nation of good-will rather than one of aggression.

And, of course, a National Service program would serve as the individual's way of saying thanks for the privilege of living in the USA.

Some readers responded to Mr. Dyckman's letter negatively, alleging that mandatory national service was an infringement on individual liberties, forgetting that we're talking about a relatively small amount of shared sacrifice. There were some very positive responses from others.

John Henningson from Guilford, CT, who served in Vietnam as a lieutenant in 1970-71, looked back on his service years as a formative time in his life when he had to address difficult challenges while working with others from very diverse backgrounds.[13]

Alison Sainsbury, Bloomington, IL, wrote that though she had lost a nephew in Afghanistan, she still felt that our present all-volunteer military has the very negative aspect of divorcing the rest of us not only from direct involvement in our wars, but even from indirect political involvement. While others are sacrificing, she added, we continue to go our way satisfying our individual needs with too little concern for the overall good of our country.[13]

Terry Maguire, a reader from Chapel Hill, NC also touched on the international element that I mentioned above when he stated that the national service program should include service worldwide. He imagined a huge nationwide network of prospects and conscripts engaged in thoughtful discussions of their plans and responsibilities as a result of participation in the program.[13]

Robert John Bennett, a *New York Times* reader living in Dusseldorf, Germany, thought Mr. Dyckman's plan requiring American youth to serve in the military or in a civilian service program made good sense and would have many benefits. However, he saw little chance of it ever being implemented in today's American social and political climate.[13]

Bennett's prediction is, in my opinion, unduly pessimistic. There is so much good about the national service idea that once people really examine its various features, once a grass roots movement gets going, the value will be hard to deny. I believe that:

- most of us need to feel pride in our country and we need a major change in how we take care of each other and of our brethren abroad

- most of us do not believe in occupying other countries where we are not welcome, or imposing our ideas of nation-building on other cultures we do not understand

and for whom our own democratic system may not be a perfect fit

- sooner or later we'll have a Congress with enough courage to do what's right for the country, not just what's right for their party

David Brooks, in his *New York Times* column "The Great Divorce" said that as we head more and more in the direction of a two-caste society described in Charles Murray's *Coming Apart,* the division and privileges of the two castes are intensified. The residential areas of the two "social tribes," as Murray describes them, in the heavily populated major cities, New York, Chicago, Dallas, and so on, are quite separate. If you are born into the upper social tribe, you will probably go to college with people of similar good fortune, marry one of the fortunate, and continue on in the same social stratum and location. You will stay in the labor force, whereas your counterpart in the lower social order has a good chance of dropping out or being rendered obsolete for lack of necessary skills.

David Brooks, in his analysis of Murray's assertions, argues that "members of the upper tribe have made themselves phenomenally productive" and "have returned to 1950s traditionalist values and practices. They have low divorce rates, arduous work ethics, and strict codes to regulate their kids." He goes on to say that "members of the lower tribe work hard and dream big, but are more removed from traditional bourgeois norms. They live in disorganized, postmodern neighborhoods in which it is much harder to be self-disciplined and productive."[14] His answer: a national service program "that would force members of the upper tribe and the lower tribe to live together, if only for a few years...a program in which people from both tribes work together to spread out the values, practices, and institutions that lead to achievement."[14]

Later in the run-up to the 2016 elections, Brooks addressed this same concern. He described the widening social divide between the well-educated with traditional family values and trust in our institutions, and the less-educated suffering from economic insecurity, broken family and community structures, and a general loss of trust. Again, one way to stop this growing separation would be through a program of national service that brings us all together.[15]

There is less social mobility in the US now than in Canada or much of Europe. And it's hard to escape one's place at the top and the bottom without radical action. Financial insecurity for a youngster is a huge challenge by itself, but it can be overcome. The insecurity that comes from a dysfunctional family where there is little love, encouragement or attention to education, is almost insurmountable.[16] What can be done about this? At present we are, if possible, making this handicap worse. Instead of major investments in social programs that could be tailored to addressing family insecurity, and strengthening the sense of worth among disadvantaged youths, we reduce taxes on the wealthy in the hope that something good will somehow trickle down to the disadvantaged. It is indeed difficult to find any evidence to support this.

Author Joseph Epstein writing in the January/February 2015 issue of *The Atlantic* said that he realized his American identity more than ever before when he quartered and shared meals as a draftee in the army. Coming from a middle class Jewish family, it was his first occasion to know American Indians, African Americans and other ethnicities of entirely different backgrounds. The experience, Epstein said, had a profound effect on his career path, encouraging him to think about what he wanted to do with his life, and helping transition him into a writing career. Epstein also noted that the draft in his era offered some young criminals military service as an alternative to reform school or prison time, and that it succeeded in starting many of them on a path to productive citizenry. Surely our National Service program would have the same effect, turning around the lives of some young gang members and other social misfits.[17]

A similar benefit was described by sociologists Sheen S. Levine and David Stark in their December 9, 2015 Op-Ed piece in *The New York Times*. They cite evidence that racial and ethnic diversity within a group makes them think more deeply about the facts of an issue or situation before they develop their opinions.[12] Isn't that what we're looking for from our fellow citizens throughout life?

Marine Vietnam War veteran and author Karl Marlantes in his *New York Times* article, "The War That Killed Trust", observed similar benefits from the diversity of military service. He thought the exposure played a significant role in fostering integration in American civilian life when the veterans came home. Marlantes described white guys being exposed to soul music for the first time, and blacks to country music. Living for an extended period of time with those of a different race promoted a range of different ideas, both good and bad, regarding racial differences, and it opened eyes to the possibility that we could, indeed, all live together in harmony.[18]

Pride in America

With all our faults, we remain the greatest nation on earth and perhaps the greatest that will ever be. As we step forward, do we not all have a duty to contribute to that legacy? However, right now, as a people, we no longer demonstrate an abundance of pride in our country's achievements, and what little we do have is surely hidden.

I am reminded of this sad fact whenever I go to a hockey game, a ball game, or a dog show (my hobby), and the band plays the national anthem as part of the opening ceremonies. While the situation has improved somewhat with the current concern for our returning warriors, many of the attendees are still too uncaring or too unpatriotic to place hand or hat over heart and look at the flag. Surely this is evidence that we have lost pride in our country or are too embarrassed by our country to display pride if we still have some. Notable exceptions are service persons, ex-service persons, or relatives of service persons; they stand tall, placing their hand or hat over their heart while looking at the flag, to remind us of what was once a common gesture. Tibetan and Chinese Monks self-immolate for what they believe in. Some extremely faithful Muslims strap bombs to themselves and commit suicide for what they believe in. And some of us can't even muster up the effort for a token display of patriotism as our flag goes by or we hear our national anthem. We have a lot of fences to mend.

While there are those that will look at these words as mere populist ramblings, read on. The sentiment is there right now to turn the unorganized actions of the OccupyWall Street or Black Lives Matter demonstrators into a revolution, hopefully one that is relatively (but not too) peaceful.

Once again, I turn to the remarks of General Stanley McChrystal in a 2013 *Wall Street Journal* opinion piece about civic duty, a responsibility he said belongs not just to the military, but to all young Americans. The general began by talking about his early lessons in citizenship, beginning with a trip he took with his father, a lieutenant colonel in the Army, to the Civil War battlefields of Gettysburg, PA. The son recalled his father talking about President Lincoln's immortal Gettysburg Address, delivered in late 1863, to memorialize the deaths of so many Union and Confederate soldiers. McChrystal's father said that Lincoln embraced a concept of citizenship in which we all follow in the footsteps of those who have gone before us in service to our country.[19] He quoted the president's ringing words about the lessons every citizen should draw from the example of the men who had died there: "It is for us the living, rather, to be dedicated to the unfinished work which they who fought here have thus far so nobly advanced."[19]

General McChrystal expressed concern with what he regarded as a neglect of citizenship exemplified by a lack of volunteers for the military. However, I contend that the nation is filled with volunteers providing all sorts of social and humanitarian services. But, we can always do better by following the words of Lincoln and dedicating ourselves to today's "unfinished work," or, as President Kennedy so aptly put it, by asking what we can do for our country.

Our National Attitude

It's time to stop blaming our problems on the Congress, the political parties, the bankers, the immigrants, Mexico, China, etc. We are not becoming a "third world" country, but, to be sure, there are many opportunities for improvement. I am absolutely certain that we can maintain and improve on our position of eminence if we stop blaming others and look to our individual selves for salvation. We have all contributed to our current malaise through envy, greed, intolerance and apathy. By embracing our fellow man, by approaching the unfamiliar in a spirit of tolerance, we can continue to do great things.

When I think of the importance of attitude, I am reminded of a quote from the evangelical Christian pastor, Charles Swindoll:

"The longer I live, the more I realize the impact of attitude on life. Attitude, to me, is more important than facts. It is more important than the past, than education, than money, than circumstances, than failures, than successes, than what other people think or say or do. It is more important than appearance, giftedness, or skill. It will make or break a company, a church, a home. The remarkable thing is we have a choice every day regarding the attitude we will embrace for that day. We cannot change our past. We cannot change the fact that people will act in a certain way. We cannot change the inevitable. The only thing we can do is play on the one string we have, and that is our attitude. I am convinced that life is

10% what happens to me and 90% how I react to it. And so it is with you, we are in charge of our attitudes."[20]

As I discuss the issues and challenges we face and my proposed National Service solution, I try to present both sides of the arguments. Where I fail, I only ask for your tolerance where we disagree. I would hope also that you are not hoping to read a left wing or right wing narrative that simply confirms biases you already hold, something we're all guilty of from time to time. As I live in New England, my main choices for written news are the *New York Times* and the *Wall Street Journal* as you will quickly learn. I have to overcome the tendency to pass by the article of a journalist with whom I generally disagree.

Then too, try to avoid the notion that a National Service program is "just one more bureaucracy" as one of my Facebook friends posted on my page. National Service will not be "just one more bureaucracy" when properly conceived and implemented.

Again, why do we need a National Service program? Let me list the reasons, many of which have been touched on already:

- In the most general terms, to end our downward social, economic and political spiral, to meet the challenges ahead, and keep America great.

- To provide our most vulnerable youth with an alternate to substance abuse and trafficking, gang membership, gun violence, radicalization by terrorist groups, and other antisocial behaviors.

- To ensure that we all have a voice in, and accept responsibility for, our political and military actions

- To build a substantial military and civilian service

resource that can respond to any threats to our nation's security, as well as to man-made and natural disasters.

- To rebuild our national pride and regain international respect,

- And most importantly, to create a better informed electorate that, through training and learning tolerance together, will understand the need for compromise at all levels of government, thereby forcing our elected officials to act and to govern accordingly

As to making "America First" again, I would argue that this cannot be done by merely protecting America's self-interests as President Donald Trump sees it, but by making America First in global leadership by

- championing freedom at home and abroad

- welcoming the politically oppressed to make a new home here in America, in the process, adding their own contributions to the nation's rich diversity

- advancing the war against poverty

- saving and protecting the planet and its resources for the use and enjoyment of all

- defeating radical Islamic Jihad and other terrorist movements

- protecting the rights of all to trade and travel freely on the high seas

Chapter Two
How Will All This Work?

The first requisite of a good citizen in this Republic of ours is that he shall be able and willing to pull his weight.

Theodore Roosevelt, New York, November 11, 1902

There are, of course, a multitude of ways in which our National Service program can be implemented. And there will be many questions and opposing views on particulars, some of which are already being discussed by proponents and opponents. Let's address some of programs suggested by others; then we'll look at my program.

Proposals by Others

Thomas Ricks, a fellow at the Center for a New American Security, expressed his views on national service in his *New York Times* article, "Let's Draft Our Kids." He states: "A revived draft, including both males and females, should include three options for new conscripts coming out of high school."[11]

Ricks proposes "18 months of military service with low pay but excellent post-service benefits, including free college tuition."[21]

(I would offer some post service benefits, but certainly not free college tuition, as I do not equate all universal service with the opportunities provided by the GI Bill following military service in time war.)

Mr. Ricks goes on to define his particular form of military service by saying that "these conscripts would not be deployed, but could perform tasks currently outsourced, at great cost to the Pentagon: paperwork, painting barracks, mowing lawns, driving generals around, and generally doing lower skill tasks so professional soldiers don't have to."[11]

As I see it, this arrangement, by creating a second, under class of military service, would defeat one of the main purposes of national service — the beneficial aspects of participating in a cadre of individuals from all social and economic classes. The service should be either military or civilian/humanitarian, but of equal value and status rather than two classes of military — "warriors" and "servants."

The question of a possible lack of *esprit de corps* comes up here. What happens when those in the two-year military element of the universal service program end up serving side by side with regular volunteer-based military personnel, some of whom might resist serving side by side with "draftees" or "conscripts"? My answer is that when the country gets on board with national service as a concept, this distinction will fade away. All will be proudly doing their duty, part of being a proud American.

Also, as indicated above, the system will be set up so that those opting for the military program as their version of national service will still have an opportunity to switch over to the regular armed forces - Army, Navy, Air Force, Marine Corps, or Coast Guard, albeit with an extended tour of duty. My system will also allow for further advance into one of the elite groups such as Special Forces, SEALs, Rangers, Recon, or Paratroops.

Thomas Ricks continues in his article, "Those who don't want to serve in the Army could perform civilian national service for a slightly longer period and equally low pay — teaching in low income areas, cleaning parks, rebuilding crumbling infrastructure, or aiding the elderly."[11]

In my view the "slightly longer period" implies that their civilian national service is less worthy than the military option, again defeating the purpose of creating a level playing field for all. No. National Service should be even-handed in its approach. For example I would offer the same post service benefits to those who have served in civilian National Service as to those who have served in military National Service. Let's rebuild our nation in every way. Let's show the world that we truly can lead, not only in our military might as we do today, but in all aspects of our social and economic values.

Ricks' third option is for the "libertarians who object to a draft." They could "opt out" but in declining to help Uncle Sam they "would in return pledge to ask nothing from him — no Medicare, no subsidized college loans and no mortgage guarantees." Ricks concludes, "Those who want minimal government can have it."[11]

Sounds nice, but, based on the framework of our current battles to provide health insurance for all, we know how this works out in reality. Notably, the uninsured, when faced with dire medical needs, go to the emergency room where their care is ultimately paid for by the taxpayer. And that's just one area of government services they inevitably come to need. I sympathize with many of the libertarians' stances, but if we really isolated the participants from all government assistance, we would surely create a new social group, akin to an "untouchable" class, one that not only included the "opt-outers" but their entire families who would become hapless "victims" of their decisions.

Here are some of the other proposals put forth both now and in the past.

William F. Buckley in his 1990 book *Gratitude — REFLECTIONS ON WHAT WE OWE TO OUR COUNTRY*[21] made a compelling case for a one-year program of civilian service primarily for 18 year-olds that, while he described it as voluntary, becomes essentially mandatory considering the benefits that he said should accrue to participants and the penalties to be imposed on those who choose not to participate. He cited President Truman's advocacy for Universal Military Training that unfortunately never came to fruition, at least not in the framework that Truman had envisioned, and he also noted that even George Washington had been an advocate for universal service. Buckley used as a basis for some of the provisions of his program Senator Sam Nunn's 1989 Citizenship and National Service Bill that offered, as a carrot to those volunteering, $10,000, in addition to ordinary living expenses, to be used for either college education or a down-payment on a mortgage.

Buckley realized, as do I, that a national service program would require a complete cultural change in America to overcome any perceived encroachment on our freedoms, but he also noted that we had been through cultural changes of similar magnitude before; for example look how far we have gone from lack of concern for our "expendable" natural resources back before Rachel Carson's time to the fierce sense of protectiveness most of us now hold for our natural environment; we have traveled much the same distance from thoughtless disrespect for the civil rights of minorities to a body of new laws protecting the rights of not only racial minorities but gender and sexual orientation minorities. Buckley also referred to the great successes enjoyed by some of our most notable volunteer service programs, for example the Peace Corps and VISTA on the national front, The Californian Conservation Corps on the state level, and the Guardian Angels in New York City on a local level.

He went into great detail on the need at that time for civilian service; the tasks were remarkably similar to today's needs: helping the elderly and handicapped, assisting in day care and schooling, maintaining parks and other public property, community cleanup, and so on.

Buckley examined all known models for a service program from a compulsory military draft to a complete voluntary system with no strings attached. His own "Buckley model" was to be administered by the individual states and overseen by a National Service Franchise Administration. While 18-year-olds were the principal target, older men and women would be welcome. A certificate of service would be provided on completion, and the individual states would determine how and when the year of service would be performed, continuous or staggered, and before, after or during college. The states would offer different service paths, for example in states such as Florida with an aging population, the focus might be more on care for and assistance to the elderly. In states with large inner city school systems, the focus might be more on helping out the teaching and administrative staff in these schools. The states would request and obtain approval from the National Service Franchise for all of their service functions, so as to set a basic standard national standard and qualify for a state certificate of service.

And here is where the carrot and the stick come in. Federal financial aid for education could be withheld from those without a certificate. Federal income taxes up to say $10,000 could be waived for those with a certificate. Colleges could be persuaded to withhold aid from those who were not graduates of national service. Those not headed for college who did not have a certificate could be subjected to other sanctions imposed by the individual state (Buckley suggested withholding drivers' licenses, but that seems too Draconian). A state that made completion of national service mandatory could then withhold a high school diploma from anyone not completing the program.

For those interested, I would strongly recommend that you read *Gratitude* (although reading Buckley can be a rather humbling experience for an amateur writer like your author). Just as in my proposed program, Buckley left most of the fine details open, but his general recommendations were quite compelling, and, as a fallback from my own mandatory program, I could accept a voluntary program with significant benefits for those participating and severe sanctions for those not.

James M. Stone is a prominent business leader and well-regarded economic thinker. In his best-selling 2016 book *5 Easy Theses - Commonsense Solutions to America's Greatest Economic Challenges,* he outlines what he calls simple solutions to America's most pressing public policy issues, from education to social and economic inequality. Discussing the challenges facing U.S. education, he claims that universal national service is the best cure. He agrees with all other proponents of national service that we owe a period of service in return for the privileges we receive from our American way of life. The benefits for the individual that he sees are exposure to the culture and opinions of others from all walks of life, and the opportunity for gaining technical training without the stigma of being put on a separate, socially unequal track from college bound students. Assuming the program is appropriately planned, there could be financial incentives for those going on to higher education, after the service is completed. Over and above these are the benefits to the nation that come from the multitude of services and talents provided by participants.

Mr. Stone traces the evolution of, and support for, national service in America, beginning with FDR's Civilian Conservation Corps and Kennedy's Peace Corps, and continuing on through

Lyndon Johnson's Head Start, Community Action and VISTA, Bill Clinton's AmeriCorps, the youth service program promoted by both President's Clinton and George H. W. Bush, and the 2009 Serve America Act supported by Senators John McCain, Orrin Hatch and Ted Kennedy that expanded AmeriCorps. But, as Stone notes, none of these really amounted to the universal national service he advocates. He proposes a one year mandatory term to be served between the ages of 17 and 22, with an option for a second year. The participant would have the choice of serving in the military (probably requiring two years), in public works and infrastructure, or in social service.

He goes into significant detail on the urgent necessity for maintenance of existing infrastructure citing the 2013 American Society of Civil Engineers report which gave failing marks to the condition of the nation's aviation facilities, dams, levees, roads, schools, transit and wastewater processing, and mediocre grades to the condition of our railroads, bridges, ports, parks and recreation facilities.

Again, unlike most of the other service programs described above by Mr. Stone, his program, like mine, is mandatory. What happens when someone refuses to enlist, you may ask. Stone is not in favor of imposing criminal penalties on objectors nor am I. Rather, he suggests sanctions generally along the lines of Mr. Buckley's. He suggests perhaps delaying social security benefits for a time equivalent to the service withheld, or denying eligibility for various government grants and subsidies.

In addressing the cost to the taxpayer of a national service program, Mr. Stone mentions a figure of $27,000 per participant that had been estimated by some opponents of universal national service, but he also noted that $16,000 was the figure generated by an Aspen Institute study. Both of these figures are significantly lower than what I have estimated in my Chapter Six. He makes the very valid point that the figures he quotes represent gross costs as do mine, and don't take into consideration the financial benefits derived from the services provided, which would likely turn the end result into a net financial benefit.

James Stone outlines other cures for our education problems, including improving the quality of high school education by adopting known "best practices" for curricula and teachers, but the best cure he sees lies in universal national service.[22]

Hillary Clinton takes a somewhat different approach. Campaigning in Ft. Pierce, Florida during the 2016 presidential campaign she proposed a National Service Reserve to be called out in times of natural disasters and other emergencies, and to meet some of our ongoing social needs. Her goal was to enlist and train five million Americans, primarily ages 18 to 30. She, like others, noted that there is a large pool of willing volunteers and that only a small portion of them can be accommodated by existing volunteer programs like the Peace Corps and AmeriCorps.

While she did not go too deeply into specifics, she sees the Reserve in the aftermath of natural disasters rebuilding homes, distributing drinking water, and generally assisting those who have become homeless. She sees those administering the program working with industry to coordinate employed individuals' work schedules with their reserve duties, and working with higher education to provide course credits for reserve experience accrued by participating high school and college students.

Secretary Clinton's Reserve is only one part of her overall national service plan. She also called for expanding AmeriCorps and the Peace Corps., as well as opportunities for meaningful service work for Senior Corps, which already has thousands of seniors 55 and older offering their time and talents.

Of course this was all presented during the campaign. It remains to be seen how much of this she will be involved in, now that she is back in private life.[23]

David Cameron, as he was approaching the end of his tenure as Britain's Prime Minister in 2016, gave what he called a "Life Chances" speech. Addressing government's role in healing some of society's ills, he wanted to expand Britain's existing voluntary National Citizen Service program for 15- to -17-year-olds as a strategy for helping to ready them for adult citizenship. The three-week program operates during summer vacation periods offering an Outward Bound style course the first week, a personal skills program the second week, and a final week in which volunteers participate directly in community service. Cameron's stated goal was to sign up 60% of 16-yr-olds to participate and to enroll 25,000 mentors to assist.[24] With Cameron's resignation after Brexit, the future of his plan to expand Britain's program is in doubt.

Still other voices in support of national service I want to mention: **Dr. Christopher B. Kuch**, a Vietnam era navy veteran and former deputy sheriff in Ohio, has suggested that, as a very minimum, a national service obligation could be a very brief stint of basic training similar to Switzerland's but even shorter. He described in *National Guard* publication a one month military indoctrination training course for all between the ages of 18 and 40 that would take place at existing military bases, National Guard facilities, recruiting centers or even at high school or local community college campuses. This would involve short courses in military operations, familiarization with weapons, understanding the chain of command, and perhaps some basic survival skills, but little if any actual physical training.[25]

Former **Maryland Governor Martin O'Malley** came out in favor of national service when he ran briefly in the Democratic presidential primaries, the only candidate on either side that did so. It would have been, should have been, an ideal debate issue.

Mayor Rahm Emanuel of Chicago mentioned the benefits gained by youngsters from diverse backgrounds working together when he advocated universal national service in an interview he gave to Chris Jones of the *Chicago Tribune* in August 2016. Emanuel stated that the country's most important step should be a three-month tour of national service after high school for all. [26]

U.S. Representatives John B. Larson (CT 01) and John Lewis (GA 05) on July 14, 2016 introduced a bill, The ACTION for National Service ACT, for a new national service plan with a goal of filling one million federal service positions with college student volunteers. These students would receive, as a reward for two years of service, compensation equal to twice the average in-state college tuition where their college is located, thereby addressing the current serious problem of student debt. The service opportunities would be in education, infrastructure, healthcare, disaster relief, and poverty.[26]

Author Sebastian Junger (*The Perfect Storm*) discussing his latest book, *Tribe*, was questioned about community building and spoke in favor of mandatory national service with both military and civilian service options.[28]

Columnist David Brooks advocates for national service frequently in his writings in The *New York Times*. .

Now, getting back to the number one advocate for national service, General McChrystal:

McChrystal's Take on National Service

General McChrystal in his previously mentioned 2013 piece in the *Wall Street Journal* offers a somewhat different approach. Rather than setting up a legally mandatory program, he suggests we develop a socially incentivizing program to create a large national service program. In this scheme, colleges and universities would adjust their student enrollment policies, and corporations their hiring practices, to benefit those who had served, effectively penalizing those who do not. In McChrystal's plan, 18- year-old men and women would be offered a choice of the five branches of the military, or several civilian service branches coordinated through AmeriCorps and other certified nonprofits, perhaps for one year, perhaps for two. Civilian service positions would be modestly paid (current AmeriCorps stipends up to $12,100 per annum are based on the federal poverty line in the region of service, plus a $5,500 scholarship bonus on completion to help with further studies). His original plan was endorsed by former Secretaries of State Condi Rice and Madeleine Albright and former Secretary of Defense Robert Gates.[29]

McChrystal adds that the demand to serve already exceeds current opportunities, with nearly 600,000 applicants applying for the 80,000 AmeriCorps positions open in 2011. Similarly, the Peace Corps receives some 150,000 requests for applications but has funding for only 4,000 new positions each year. McChrystal sees this as a huge waste of the talents and patriotism of our young men and women, our most precious resource. And what a waste it is. In his nearly four decades in the military, the general saw the priceless benefits gained by our young as a result of serving in the military in peacetime as well as wartime. Working in challenging circumstances with colleagues of many different backgrounds, they received valuable lessons in discipline and teamwork and, for some, the basics of leadership.[19]

McChrystal anticipates, as do I, that however such a program is

organized — whether by legal mandate or through social inducements, its implementation will be an uphill battle. But he is convinced, as am I, that we need this type of effort, indeed *national
service*, in order to help accomplish some of our major national
goals: reducing the high-school dropout rate, conserving our rivers, lakes, and parks, preparing for and responding to natural and
man-made disasters, and reducing poverty.[19]

As McChrystal points out, there is a huge pool of willing applicants out there. The Aspen Institute's Franklin Project, now part
of The Service Year Alliance on whose board he serves as chairman, identifies a comparably huge pool of 501(c)(3) charities
who require the services of these volunteers and who are in a position to provide some compensation to them for their services.
The goal of Service Year Alliance is, of course, to bring these two
groups together.

There are a myriad of other opportunities to volunteer for community or national service, many of which are sponsored by and
can be researched by visiting the Corporation for National and
Community Service on the web, www.nationalservice.gov.

President Obama in July 2013 created a task force to expand national service "through partnerships to advance government priorities." In his memorandum, he stated that "Service has always
been integral to the American identity. Our country was built on
the belief that all of us, working together, can make this country
a better place for all. That spirit remains as strong and integral
to our identity today as at our country's founding. Since its creation 20 years ago, the Corporation for National and Community
Service (CNCS) has been the federal agency charged with leading and expanding national service. The Edward M. Kennedy
Serve America Act of 2009 (SAA) expanded CNCS's authority
to create opportunities for more Americans to serve. This landmark, bipartisan legislation focuses national service on six areas:

emergency and disaster service; economic opportunity; education; environmental stewardship; healthy futures; and veterans and military families....National service and volunteering can be effective solutions to national challenges....Americans are ready and willing to serve. Applications from Americans seeking to engage in national service programs far exceed the number of available positions. By creating new partnerships between agencies and CNCS that expand national service opportunities in areas aligned with agency missions, we can utilize the American spirit to improve lives and communities, expand economic and educational opportunities, enhance agencies' capacity to achieve their missions, efficiently use tax dollars, help individuals develop skills that will enable them to prepare for long-term careers, and build a pipeline to employment inside and outside the Federal Government."[30]

All of this brings to mind one of President George H. W. Bush's finest legacies, his "Thousand Points of Light" Inaugural Address, in which he invoked the vision of a nation served by countless citizens seeing a need, in effect lighting a candle, and stepping forward to aid their fellow Americans. From that speech came the Points of Light Institute, which was set up to champion the contributions, no matter how small, made by millions of anonymous citizens.

Then too, for those interested in volunteering for international service, there are many unique opportunities offered by United Nations Volunteers (UNV). The importance of participating in these programs is recognized by The President's Council on Service and Civic Participation through their President's Volunteer Service Award.

My Broader Definition of National Service

My program is very comprehensive, and it is mandatory rather than voluntary for a variety of reasons that will become clear, not the least of which is the fact that a voluntary program would likely elude those who would most benefit from it. I am proposing a traditional military type draft in which everyone, on reaching their 18th birthday, is eligible for, and will eventually be chosen for, the draft. Those in their fourth year of high school (possibly those coming of age in their third year also) would be allowed to defer assignment until completion of their fourth year, with or without a high school diploma.

The service period would start out with basic military training, i.e. boot camp, for all . The boot camp would be essentially identical to that used for current army inductees. This would ensure the maximum force of available personnel equipped with basic military training in the event of a long-term major conflict or other national emergency so that we would always have a pool of physically able youth to fill the military needs. Today, by contrast, it is estimated that 70 percent of our youth are not physically eligible to serve. Unfortunately, a lot has changed in the physical condition of our youth since the days of Pearl Harbor when we were able to rapidly mobilize our military and prepare for war. The nature and reasons for this disparity are variously described as asthma, obesity, cutbacks in school physical education requirements, and lack of exercise resulting from time spent on iPhones, computers and TV.[31]

Upon completion, the draftee could elect and be assigned to military-type service or civilian service. This latter could be either national social work or international humanitarian aid work.

National Social Work could include:

- Assisting in school classrooms in low-income areas

- Providing support and guidance for disadvantaged youth

- Providing maintenance, cleanup and other tasks in national parks

- Repairing and rebuilding failing infrastructure

- Aiding welfare recipients and the elderly, handicapped and homebound

- Responding to natural and man-made disasters

- Cleaning up lakes and waterways

- Urban renewal in low-income neighborhoods

- Preservation work at historic sites

- Restoring national forests and eroded coastal dunes

- Assisting in border patrol (shared with the military)

- Assisting disabled and/or homeless veterans

- Assisting in vetting refugees and immigrants

International Social Work could include:

- Building schools

- Digging wells, irrigation systems and community gardens

- Teaching safety and health

- Vaccinating people and livestock

- Road building in remote areas

- Disaster recovery

- Refugee monitoring and support at international camps

The Pentagon, with Congressional approval, would determine the numerical strength required by the military, including those in the National Service program, those who are career military, those who opt for an additional military term(s) after completing their compulsory National Service, and those serving in the National Guard/Reserves.

Incidentally, the National Guard/Reserves would be significantly altered based on a variety of redundancies that might exist after creation of the National Service program. Quite likely, the National Service program would even replace the National Guard/Reserves as it would have sufficient conscripts to assign to the duties currently handled by the Guard and Reserves. If the numerical requirements are not met voluntarily, then the military would have first priority in filling its ranks from among the National Service program conscripts. Only after that would the option to choose civilian service be available.

A general educational element as described in Chapter Eleven would follow the basic military training. The advantage of implementing this early in the National Service tour instead of at the end is that the remainder of the tour will give ample opportunity to discuss the subjects with colleagues and to take advantage of the written handouts and books on the course reading lists. The curriculum would cover those life skills not taught, or inadequately taught, in either a trade school or academic track in secondary education, and would be designed to prepare students to survive and even prosper in the increasingly challenging socio-economic climate of our time. Courses would include:

- Civics

- Introduction to taxes, health insurance, and retirement benefits

- Economic theories

- Personal money matters

- Lessons in international understanding

and a variety of other life preparation courses

An appropriate additional period of education or skills training specific to the task assigned would follow that, as for example, infantry or artillery training for some of those in the military service, or possibly some computer literacy training for some of those in the civilian service component. Our community colleges could play a role here. After skills training specific to the task, the final assignment, military or civilian service, would commence.

Eighteen-year-olds will still have the opportunity to pre-empt the "draft" by enlisting for a longer period in a military branch of their choice, to become a regular member of the Army, Navy, Marine Corps, Air Force, or Coast Guard. Those who are considering the military as a career would probably opt for this. And this brings up a question about the above-mentioned educational element of our program. As all of our conscripts will be taking advantage of this, should it also be part of our regular military training? I would think yes, but a case could be made either way. Perhaps it could be evaluated in the National Service program and, if deemed advantageous to do so, added to the regular military program at a later time.

Discipline and Enforcement

Following publication of his *Coming Apart*, author Charles Murray, responding to a reader's concerns, addressed national service and the issues of discipline and enforcement. The reader had complained that Murray was generous in citing problems with American society but did not offer any solutions. Murray grudgingly agreed in a subsequent column he wrote in the *New York Times* entitled "Narrowing the New Class Divide." But, he added, "Solutions that are remotely practicable right now would not do much good."[32]

He went on to give a case in point:

"The solution I hear proposed most often [is] a national service program that would bring young people of all classes together…. The precedent, I am told, is the military draft, which ended in the early 1970s. But the draft was able to shape unwilling draftees into competent soldiers because Army officers had the Uniform Code of Military Justice to make their orders stick."[32]

"Administrators of a compulsory civilian national service program would likewise face young people who mostly didn't want to be there," Murray continues, but "without being able to enforce military-style discipline, such a program would replicate the unintended effect of jobs programs for disadvantaged youth in the 1970s: training young people how to go through the motions and beat the system. National service would probably create more resentment than camaraderie."[32]

I totally disagree. I'm talking about a complete change in culture that will encourage people to serve, to do their part. Peer pressure will be a factor. The military element of the program will function essentially the same as it does now, except that it will apply to conscripts as well as volunteers. Military-style discipline based on the Uniform Code of Military Justice will continue to be the rule.

A disciplinary code will also be developed for the civilian part of the program, somewhat more lenient than the military code because the national security aspect critical to military service is not an issue. It must still be rigorous enough to ensure that the goals of the program are met. Civilian National Service is not going to be "fun and games at Camp Feelgood." While the Pentagon and the Department of Defense will be responsible for overseeing and administering the boot camp and the military component that follows, the education element and civilian service component will be under the control of a new department headed by a new Cabinet member, or possibly by a new bureau under the umbrella of an existing department, possibly State or Education

I would expect that some of the phases of a service involved in humanitarian aid, for example, would have recourse to disciplinary action when appropriate, because service people under this umbrella are acting as good-will ambassadors for all of us. Other phases — conservation work, for example — would function more as a "team effort" with management by consensus. With a certain amount of trial and error, the right balance of discipline and team consensus can be achieved for all components of National Service.

It is not my intent to work out all the details here. Suffice to say that, when this program comes about, all of us who support the idea will work diligently to smooth its way through legislative passage with provisions that minimize government bureaucracy and waste.

One very obvious question that I leave unanswered, even unaddressed, is how and when the program should include women. At a Senate hearing in May 2016, General Robert Neller, the Commandant of the Marine Corps, General Mark Milley, the Army Chief of Staff, and Patrick Murphy, the Acting Secretary of the Army, all encouraged the Senate to investigate a requirement for women to register for the draft.[33] And in 2016 as an indication of the positive role women can play in the military, Capt. Kristen Griest , one of the first women to graduate from the storied Army Ranger School also became the first woman to lead an infantry combat unit.[34]

This being so, the National Service draft should apply to men and women from the outset. However, logistics and practicality issues may require further study to resolve how best to achieve this. What would be the effect on the work force remaining if nearly 100 percent of young men and women in this age group were suddenly removed for two years from entering the conventional job market? How would our institutions of higher learning adjust their programs and operating budgets if hundreds of thousands of college-bound draftees were simultaneously forced to postpone enrollment until they completed their service?

One solution might be to start by conscripting men only, but with a provision for women to volunteer at a later date. As the program and the nation became accustomed to the idea, mandatory service for women could be phased in. Accordingly, logistics and practicality issues could outweigh any potential discrimination issues. Another possibility would be to phase in the program over three to five years, during which time we would fill the rolls by lottery with both men and women.

Chapter Three
Our Decline

The tree of liberty must be refreshed from time to time with the blood of patriots and tyrants. It is its natural manure.

Thomas Jefferson letter to W.S. Smith November 13, 1787

Our position as leader of the free world has been declining for several decades, and, unless we make revolutionary changes that other great empires could never quite achieve, we will soon become just another second-rate power in a world where many nations are constantly jockeying for some short-term gain.

The American Empire

When we speak of empires, Americans tend to think of the Roman Empire, the British Empire, perhaps the Ottoman Empire and the Austro-Hungarian Empire, even the old Soviet Union. All these empires are has-beens, having lost their way and their wealth through their inability to keep reimagining themselves and their institutions. We do not see ourselves in this company. But make no mistake; we have been a great empire-builder since the days of our migration westward from the original 13 Colonies. Our ambitions have brought us the Louisiana Purchase, the Texas

Annexation, the Mexican Cession, the annexations of California, Oregon, and Alaskan territories, Teddy Roosevelt's Cuban foray, our creation of the Panama Canal Zone, and our Pacific adventures in Hawaii and the Philippines.

After World War II, we continued our expansion into Asia through the occupation of a defeated Japan (justifiably so) and our efforts at controlling the destiny of the Korean Peninsula. We complemented these moves with the Marshall Plan. And in the process of rebuilding Western Europe, we created a massive trading partner and provided a bulwark against the expansionist aims of the Soviet Union. We continue to have an overt military presence throughout the Pacific basin and Europe, and a vast array of military or intelligence involvement — some covert, some very visible — throughout the Middle East, Africa, Central America, and virtually every other part of the world. Can this go on, or will we, like the great empires before us, decline?

Our "American Empire" will only survive this century if it is based on positive motives and mutual good. It must encompass the spread of freedom, humanitarian aid where needed, and global trade that benefits our partners as well as ourselves. In the new global economy, the traditional imperial posture — military supremacy, political governance, and trade advantages — no longer works nor should it.

As Winston Churchill reputedly once said, "America always manages to get it right after they've tried everything else." I think we've now pretty much tried everything else. We must now redefine our vision. We must reclaim our democratic heritage with all Americans participating in how we run our affairs. We cannot leave it to our military, nor our politicians, nor our corporate interests speaking through their lobbyists. All of us must take responsibility for our future, rededicating ourselves to a common purpose through a national service program.

The Fragility of Democratic Institutions

The disquieting words, generally attributed to 18th-century Scottish history professor Alexander Fraser Tytler, bear repeating here. About the fall of the Athenian Republic in the fourth century BC, he supposedly declared, "A democracy is always temporary in nature; it simply cannot exist as a permanent form of government. A democracy will continue to exist up until the time that voters discover that they can vote themselves generous gifts from the public treasury. From that moment on, the majority always votes for the candidates who promise the most benefits from the public treasury, with the result that every democracy will finally collapse over loose public policy, [which is] always followed by a dictatorship."[35]

Also attributed to Tytler is a way of seeing history as a repeating pattern of progress and decline. The so-called "Tytler Cycle" holds that "the average age of the world's greatest civilizations from the beginning of history has been about 200 years." During those 200 years these nations, when the people can no longer tolerate their condition and start to resist, "always progressed through the following sequence:

> From bondage to spiritual faith;
>
> From spiritual faith to great courage;
>
> From courage to liberty;
>
> From liberty to abundance;
>
> From abundance to complacency;
>
> From complacency to apathy;
>
> From apathy to dependence;
>
> From dependence back into bondage."[35]

From where did we come and where do we stand now in America's cycle. Surely we started to rise out of "bondage" to Britain's King George when the Sons of Liberty dumped tea into Boston Harbor as a protest against unfair taxation in 1773. Surely, we saw our way forward when the Minutemen drove the Red Coats back at "the rude bridge that arched the flood" in Concord, Massachusetts in 1775. Spiritual faith animated the authors of the Declaration of Independence when in the following year they gathered in Philadelphia to pledge to one another their lives, fortunes, and sacred honor "with a firm reliance on the protection of Divine Providence" and to declare that their "United Colonies are and ought to be free and independent States."

The hardships and "courage" of the Continental Army brought the first taste of "liberty" when General George Washington accepted Lord Cornwallis' sword in surrender after the battle of Yorktown in 1781. But true "liberty" did not arrive until seven years later in 1788 when the Constitution of the United States of America was ratified and three years later in 1791 when the first ten amendments, The Bill of Rights, were added, guaranteeing the freedoms that have been the foundation of our national values ever since.

Over the subsequent two centuries we experienced "abundance" unprecedented as we rode the waves of the industrial and technological revolutions, raising the living standards of all our people. Now, however, our economy has not only stalled, but it has been slipping backward, suffering in the aftermath of the Great Recession of 2009. Our completely dysfunctional government has been unable or unwilling to take the hard steps necessary to get us back on track. Too many of us who still have a comfortable standard of living are "complacent." Too many of those living in poverty, have given up fighting "the system," settling in to a life of dependence on subsidies from state and federal governments. It would seem that in this second decade of the 21st century we are as a nation somewhere between Tytler's "complacency" and "apathy," or in some cases somewhere between "apathy" and "dependence." If so, our best days are long past and we are heading, in all probability, back to "bondage." Rather than stand by passively, let us resolve right now to select a new and more positive path for America.

The impetus for change must come from the bottom up, from the voters. Based on our current experience, we surely cannot expect our elected officials to take the lead by offering fresh ideas. The old politics have got them where they are. Their overwhelming focus these days is on re-election. However, putting our faith solely in "the bottom" is problematic. Our "bottom" has not so far demonstrated the capacity to effect the change we need.

I contend that the root cause of this incapacity is a lack of adequate education. I'm referring not only to a lack of traditional learning according to a core curriculum; I am equally concerned that too many of the electorate have little or no exposure to the principles and values that have made equal opportunity a cornerstone of our way of life. This exposure — call it civics training if you like — should and will be a key element of the training phase of our National Service program.

We all understand that many of the jobs that kept America at near full employment for so long have been lost in recent decades and are not coming back. The replacement of human labor with the machines of mass production and the digital revolution, as well as globalization that has allowed us to outsource many jobs to lower-paid workers around the world, are largely to blame. But we cannot ignore the toll that our failing education system and our high rate of high school drop outs are taking on our productivity. Other more ambitious nations are seizing the opportunities while we affix blame everywhere but on ourselves.

Nowhere is the cyclical transition "from apathy to dependence" more evident than in the plight of the impoverished minorities living in the shameful ghettos of some of our major cities. Here, where government should create subsidized enterprise zones attracting job-producing factories, there is nothing but despair and indifference. These conditions have led to what is commonly known as a "culture of poverty," typical examples of which can be found in urban minority communities where broken families, welfare dependency, and a feeling of helplessness, and illicit drugs prevail.[36] Those entrepreneurs with enough energy and ambition within this culture find that their best route to prosperity is by selling the most readily available, most sought after product in their environment: illicit drugs. We cannot as a nation allow this pathology to continue. It can and must be fixed. And it will be, when we each shoulder our share of the work.

Step forward, America

Let's be the only empire that doesn't self-destruct. I'm not ready to surrender to a world dominated by China or a Pan-Islamic federation, or a global network of industrial oligarchs plundering the earth with allegiances only to themselves and their own greedy goals.

The basic tenets on which the United States was founded are still vital to our sense of national purpose, but they may not be sufficient to guide us in the modern era. James Gustave Speth writing in his manifesto *America the Possible* thinks not. He sees a compelling need now for a "separation of corporation and state"[37] equal to the need for a "separation of church and state" foreseen by our founders. Speth says that this cutting of the ties between corporation and state will come about not by diminishing the power of the corporation but by redirecting it: "The corporation that offers the best hope for the future is one that prioritizes public benefit over private profit, that is locally rooted and faithful to its employees and its communities, and that ensures these objectives will be met through more democratic patterns of ownership and management."[38]

Socialism? No! This change in American culture can be accomplished when an enlightened electorate *protects* the resources of production, keeping them in the private sector. But that private sector must then redirect its concern for investor profits to one that shapes policy on the basis of what is best for all. That very same culture is found in our military now; and it is replicable in our National Service program in the future.

What are Our Shortcomings and Challenges?

- **Inequality of opportunity between the upper educated class and the lower poorly educated class:** We are making some inroads in combatting the worst immediate effects of inequality, which is homelessness. Family homelessness is down significantly and veteran homelessness is down even more. Two states — Virginia and Connecticut — have essentially eliminated veteran homelessness. President Obama in 2016 proposed $11 billion over 10 years to make further gains.[39]

  But longer term permanent solutions to inequality lie in fixing the causes, not just the symptoms, and that's a big challenge.

  Education and training are major sticking points in enabling the working class to move up the economic ladder. The increasing inequality of opportunity between the upper educated classes and the lower poorly educated is caused in part by technological advances that favor highly-trained workers. New office jobs require more skills and thus more specialized education, which inevitably favors those who can afford such training.

Also contributing to inequality are global trade, which puts downward pressure on the wages of the working class, and the failure of trade union leaders to exercise a positive influence. Market forces induce private industry to outsource jobs globally in pursuit of greater profit, thereby contracting rather than expanding job opportunities at home.

And, of course, Jobs must be created for those who have been replaced by robots and other technologically-based efficiencies.

- **<u>Corporate and special interest money play too large a role in guiding legislative outcomes.</u>** Thanks to a controversial decision made by the Supreme Court in 2005 regarding Citizens United vs. the Federal Elections Commission, the legal floodgates have opened to allow huge amounts of money from undisclosed sources such as corporations to pour into super PACs or political action committees for the purposes of influencing elections and government legislation. The justices' majority opinion was that corporations, like individuals, are entitled to the protection of the First Amendment and that their donations were a form of free speech. This is, not only in my opinion but in the opinion of many Constitutional experts — a horribly misguided interpretation of one of our most precious Constitutional rights, with the potential to skew virtually every vote cast by our policy makers.

- **<u>Unequal Justice:</u>** Massachusetts Senator Elizabeth Warren, a consistent advocate for economic reform in government and big business, released a report in 2016 concerning corporate misconduct and the failure of our financial watchdogs to adequately intercept such gross lapses or prosecute those responsible. She cited as examples the scores of bankers who sold inflated home mortgages to consumers clearly unequipped by income or history to carry such debts, with the result that tens of thousands were thrust into personal bankruptcy and homelessness. She named several of the nation's biggest banks that had directly profited from policies that brought on the 2008 financial collapse, including JP Morgan Chase, Wells Fargo, Goldman Sachs, Bank of America, and UBS, listing such shadowy practices as money laundering, tax evasion, and currency manipulation. She said that the government's several oversight agencies had also failed, on the "too big to fail" theory that to do so would cause greater disruptions. She noted that few were charged for anything, and when penalties *were* applied, they were modest fines with no jail time.

Warren also went after the large-for-profit colleges like Education Management Corporation, for defrauding thousands of students seeking to upgrade their job skills by lying about course offerings, employing un-credentialed instructors, awarding useless degrees, and leaving the majority of enrollees stuck with unmanageable student debt. She shamed Novartis, a major international pharmaceutical manufacturer, for paying illegal kickbacks to doctors to promote high-priced drugs to patients who could ill afford them.

Surely when we are all better educated to the workings of our government and corporate America, we will demand that our legislators and our watchdogs do a better job of ensuring equal justice and punishment when warranted for all, and not just when robbers and drug dealers in urban ghettoes are in their crosshairs, as it is now.[40]

- **Our nation lacks a clearly understood comprehensive foreign policy or "mission,"** so that our leaders, when faced with uprisings and/or other threats such as those emanating from the Middle East, Ukraine, or North Korea, for example, don't have any firm guidelines on when and why we should go to war. This is addressed later in this chapter under **The Absence of a Non-Partisan Foreign Policy.**

Paying for Our Sins/Excesses

There is a downside to the liberty that we all enjoy. Kurt Anderson in an opinion piece in the *New York Times* claims that "from the beginning, the American idea embodied a tension between radical individualism and the demands of the commonweal...."life, liberty, and the pursuit of happiness' — individualism in a nutshell."[40] He says Thomas Jefferson was aware of this and warned against the pitfalls of "self love." Anderson goes on to argue that the so-called Gilded Age of the last quarter of the nineteenth century and the Roaring Twenties of the twentieth century were periods when we went "overboard indulging our propensities to self-gratification."[40] Thanks to various crises, Anderson explains, we managed to extricate ourselves and come out for the better in both instances. "Then came the late 1960s, and over the next two decades American individualism was fully unleashed .... Going forward, the youthful masses of every age would be permitted as never before to indulge their self-expression and hedonistic impulses."[41]

Anderson continues, "the self-absorbed 'Me' Decade, having expanded during the 1980s and '90s from personal life to encompass the political economy, will soon be the 'Me' Half-Century."[40] Pessimistic perhaps, but I share his concern. Individually we take from society more than we give, living beyond our means and pretending that it is our right to do so. Under National Service this will change: with every member of society in some way engaged in the service ideal, there will be much more exposure to and empathy for others from all walks of life.

We have built our prosperity as a nation, and as individuals, to a large extent on debt, and we are passing our excessive expenditures and habits of wastefulness on to future generations. Much of the current talk about the decline of the middle class is a miscalculation of what is really happening. Yes, some of us are experiencing a decline in income and financial security, but the decline is from artificial levels of prosperity and perceived "need" that in many cases were unearned to begin with. Our life styles no longer equate to the labors that get us there: two or more automobiles in the driveway, two or three TVs in the house, all sorts of iPads, computers, iPhones, game consoles, lawn and pool services, a couple of annual cruises or other vacations, frequent dine-outs, and clothes that are discarded as out-of-fashion after a few uses. (If you doubt this, go look at what ordinary folks donate by the armload to Goodwill Industries and thrift shops to see how extravagant this habit has become).

The middle class, as well as the rich, have been accustomed to thinking that we deserve all these goodies due to our years of hard work. Yet, for many, the work is not really "hard." Rather it is doing that for which we have a passion. This goes for investment bankers, high tech engineers, fund managers, management consultants, athletes, physicians, entertainers and so on. Their efforts may be diligent, productive, even admirable…but "hard", no. Hard work is digging ditches, felling trees, doing construction work and other manual labor, doing what we need to survive and to feed our family, no matter how arduous and unpleasant.

Let's start earning a different kind of prosperity — one that we can truly pay for and from which we can gain personal satisfaction through service to others and therefore to our country. We should never forget the often-quoted words of President Kennedy in his first inaugural speech: "Ask not what your country can do for you. Ask what you can do for your country." And so I come back to the opportunities for personal betterment to be found in a program of universal service. Every National Service participant will have the opportunity to make a meaningful contribution that will remain a source of pride for life. And as they go on to productive careers they can also look back on their tours of duty knowing that they have been given a good foundation on which to build.

Losing Face, Losing Place

What has our habit of spending beyond our means really bought us besides worry and financial insecurity? Not much. *New York Times* Columnist Charles Blow put it in stark terms, writing "It's time for us to stop lying to ourselves about this country. America is great in many ways, but on a whole host of measures ... we have become the laggards of the industrialized world. Not only are we not No. 1 — 'U.S.A.! U.S.A.!' — we are among the worst of the worst."

He compares us on various social and economic measures to the rest of the 33 International Monetary Fund's advanced economies. While we score reasonably well in such democratic institutions as electoral process and pluralism, civil liberties, and political participation, and we rate reasonably well in the Gallup Global Wellbeing Index and in student performance in science, we trail in far too many other critical metrics.

For example, with regard to income inequality only Singapore, Hong Kong, and Switzerland show a greater divide between rich and poor.

In food insecurity, a measure based on the frequency with which survey families reported not having enough money to buy the food they needed some days of the month, we rank among the most insecure.

In life expectancy at birth, we rank in 27th position, with only six of the 33 countries having a lower expectancy.

In the percentage of our population in prison, we occupy the bottom rung, with 743 of every 100,000 citizens incarcerated.

In student performance in math, we are down at 29th position, with only four of the 33 countries below us.[42]

James Speth in his *America the Possible* found similar poor performances when the U.S. is compared to the 20 other leading democracies that make up the Organization for Economic Cooperation and Development (OECD), including the United Kingdom, France, Germany, the Nordic countries, Japan, Canada, and others. Writing in 2012, he found that "America now has:

- The highest poverty rate, both generally and for children;

- The greatest inequality of income;

- The lowest government spending as a percentage of gross domestic product (GDP) on social programs for the disadvantaged;

- The lowest score on the United Nations' index of 'material well-being of children';

- The worst score on the United Nations' gender inequality index;

- The lowest social mobility;

- The highest public and private expenditure on health care as a percentage of GDP, and yet the highest infant mortality rate, prevalence of mental health problems, obesity rate, percentage of people going without health care due to cost concerns, and consumption of antidepressants per capita, along with the shortest life expectancy at birth;

- The third lowest scores for student performance in math, and middling scores in science and reading;

- The second highest high school dropout rate;

- The highest homicide rate;

- The largest prison population both absolute and per capita;

- The highest water consumption per capita and the second highest carbon dioxide emissions per capita;

- The lowest score on the Yale — World Economic Forum's Environmental Performance Index, and the second largest ecological footprint per capita;

- The highest rate of failing to ratify international agreements;

- The third lowest spending on international development and humanitarian assistance as a percentage of GDP;

- The highest military spending in total and as a percentage of GDP;

- The largest international arms sales."[43]

Yes, there are extenuating circumstances in our sub-par performances on a few of these, as in in our high military spending stemming from our role as international protectors of not only ourselves but of many of our OECD peers. Nevertheless, the overall pattern is disturbing.

Speth's analysis of our social well-being brings me back to two of the shortcomings and challenges I listed earlier in this chapter. They were inequality of opportunity and the excessive influence of corporate and special interest money on social and economic policy.

The Absence of a Non-Partisan Foreign Policy

One issue that is not included in Speth's analysis is our country's lack of a full-fledged foreign policy that would give guidance to our leaders when they must wrestle with how best to respond to foreign aggression. .

When we do go to war, we go with one hand tied behind our back, because we do not have the fiscal courage to fund these efforts adequately. We take barely enough troops into battle, provide them with insufficient protective equipment, and instruct them to conduct what is in effect a holding pattern while we try to reach diplomatic solutions We therefore never come out truly victorious, and we never settle the issue in a way that permanently ends the threat that brought us into war. Witness the military engagements in Korea, Vietnam, Iraq, and Afghanistan.

As James Fallows pointed out in "The Tragedy of the American Military" in *The Atlantic,* with all the money spent in Iraq our only lasting strategic success was the killing of Osama bin Laden. Our other victories there, ridding Iraq of Saddam Hussein and joining forces with Sunni tribal leaders, for example, did not give us a lasting peace. Fallows thinks lack of funding is not the problem. Rather, our leaders lack the resolve to reform Pentagon management or craft a a more modern weapons program. Ten years after the 9/11 attacks President Obama authorized a bipartisan commission to investigate waste and duplication in the Department of Defense. Among the commission's findings was that methods of procurement and contracting had little or no oversight or objective auditing, with the result that spending on defense and security had increased 96% in the single decade. Unfortunately, Obama never pursued the commission's recommendations, not even the one that called for appointment of a task force to assess the costly mistakes that had been made in the long wars in Afghanistan and Iraq in order to learn from them.[44] In the 2012 presidential campaign that followed, neither Obama nor his opponent, Mitt Romney offered any details on how our military funding could be better applied.

Mr. Fallows recommends that only through modernizing our weapons programs and funding a universal army such as I and others have been describing will we be able in the future to assemble quickly the overwhelming manpower necessary to truly strike, shock, and defeat our enemies into unconditional surrender. Never again should we put "boots on the ground" in a real or shadow war without the intention to defeat the enemy and along with our allies to occupy their territory long enough to satisfy our goals. Typical of these situations would be immediate threats to ourselves or others from non-state groups committing acts of genocide and other atrocities. The Islamic State of Iraq and Syria (ISIS) and Boko Haram would fall into this category. Their violent barbaric actions are so egregious that the civilized world cannot simply stand back and ignore them. These organizations must be eradicated. Where do we see adversaries crossing the line into this category? Well, this would seem to be a case of "we can't define it, but we know it when we see it." Speaking in Havana March 21, 2016 President Obama said "We will defeat those who threaten the safety and security of people all around the world",[45] following up by saying that defeating ISIS was his "top priority", and President Trump has repeated the call by pledging in his inaugural speech to "eradicate them from the face of the earth".

There are of course some exceptions to the above such as short-term engagements when we are called upon to supply humanitarian aid, as after the Phuket, Thailand, tsunami in 2004 and the Haitian earthquake in 2010.

However, there are some who disagree with the maintenance of a large global military presence as required to meet the above needs. I refer to military historian Andrew Bacevich, cited by Speth in his *America the Possible*. Bacevich, a professor of history and international relations at Boston University, "sees the current U.S. military posture as a product of a 'sacred trinity': 'An abiding conviction that the minimum essentials of international peace and order require the United States to maintain a global military presence, to configure its forces for global power projection, and to counter existing or anticipated threats by relying on a policy of global interventionism.' "[46]

However, he takes issue with this current U.S. posture. He offers instead "a new set of Washington rules: 'First, the purpose of the U.S. military is not to combat evil or remake the world, but to defend the United States and its most vital interests….The United States should maintain only those forces required to accomplish [this] core mission. Second, the primary duty station of the American soldier is in America. Just as the U.S. military should not be a global police force, so too it should not be a global occupation force….Third, consistent with the Just War tradition, the United States should employ force only as a last resort and only in self-defense.' "[45]

Based on current world events I see Bacevich's "new set of Washington rules" as wishful thinking. When required to act, to go to war, our force should be overwhelming, as well as capable of a response totally disproportionate to the enemy's unprovoked actions, to ensure that the engagement is as brief as possible and decisive. In the immortal words of Teddy Roosevelt, we should "speak softly and carry a big stick." And it should be a very big stick, including as an essential component the military piece of our National Service program.

As we watched the ease with which Russia invaded and absorbed the neighboring Crimean peninsula and the subsequent massive buildup of their troops along the southern and eastern borders of Ukraine, most of us came to realize that we were once again in a helpless position. There was no way to respond militarily, and it was quite obvious that Vladimir Putin was counting on our inaction before he made his move. Our military forces were overcommitted elsewhere in Afghanistan, in other parts of the Middle East, and in Southeast Asia. Without an excess of available military personnel, we could not support militarily any nation not included under the NATO umbrella.

This incident was an eye-opener for us, even a reason to reassess our current military posture, which relies on an overall reduction in personnel and a focus on smaller highly specialized and highly mobile strike forces strategically placed. Based on our concerns with the volatility in the Middle East and other international hot spots, this revised focus might seem to be appropriate. However, it now appears that the Cold War may not actually be over. Apparently we still may need the ability to mass large numbers of troops along the borders of some of our NATO allies, for example Poland and the Baltic States, to discourage Mr. Putin from further aggression. We have made a start in this direction with the addition of a small military presence there.

Our National Service program troops could be a vital part of this expanded force, certainly in support roles, and probably also in front line duty. To any concerns the reader might raise regarding the sufficiency of training proposed for National Service troops as compared with regular enlistees, realize that many recruits with less than two years' active service have traditionally performed admirably in most of our past conflicts. Since the end of the original Cold War, we have seen a general decline in the capability of the Russian military when compared to that at the height of the Soviet Union. Even given the reports that the training, quality, and capabilities of the Russian soldier have improved over the past few years, there is no reason to believe that our National Service program military element would not be a match for them.

While military capability and strength must be a key element of our global leadership, we must also remember, as noted Libertarian Ron Paul said, that "setting a good example is a far better way to spread ideals than through force of arms."[47] Paul added, "We have a lot of goodness in this country. And we should promote it, but never through the barrel of a gun. We should do it by setting good standards, motivating people, and having them want to emulate us."[47] I share Paul's optimism, but let's keep "the barrel of a gun" always ready, just in case!

With the wars in the Middle East, the nuclear agreement with Iran, and the threats posed by a nuclear-armed and pugnacious North Korea, the question of when to use "the barrel of a gun" has come under close scrutiny with some very strong arguments that our leaders have become too hesitant to use military force. It is understandable that we have become extremely reluctant to engage militarily after so many years fighting in Afghanistan and Iraq with no clear-cut victory, no compelling positive results, enormous budgetary impact and untold military and civilian casualties on both sides. In March 2016 Jim Himes, Representative from the 4th Connecticut District, made some interesting comments to his constituency that we could all heed. He implied that before we seriously consider scrapping the Iran nuclear agreement, or militarily confronting Russia in Ukraine or China in the South China Sea, we should take a hard look at the consequences of military intervention versus diplomatic negotiations. Congressman Himes addressed the costly disasters of our interventions in Iraq and Libya (Afghanistan?) and the similarly disastrous outcomes in Syria where, to the dismay of President Obama's critics, we chose not intervene. The lesson Himes offers is that, whether or not we intervene militarily has little effect when compared with diplomatic negotiations on the eventual outcomes.[48] This lesson should be incorporated in the foreign policy course given to National Service recruits , described in greater detail in Chapter Eleven.

Chapter Four

Rethinking Our Educational System from a Global Perspective

> *Education is the most powerful weapon which you can use to change the world*
>
> *Nelson Mandela — speech Boston June 23, 1990*

In Tom Friedman's *New York Times* column "Pass the Books. Hold the Oil," he quotes Andreas Schleicher, director of the Program for International Student Assessment (PISA) for the Organization for Economic Cooperation and Development. Schleicher observes that "today's learning outcomes at school are a powerful predictor for the wealth and social outcomes that countries will reap in the long run."[48] He cites as excellent examples Finland, Singapore, Hong Kong, South Korea, and Japan, all countries with few natural resources. In those countries "education has strong outcomes and a high status, at least in part because the public at large has understood that the country must live by its knowledge and skills and that these depend on the quality of its education....Every parent and child in these countries knows that these skills will decide the life chances of the child and nothing else is going to rescue them, so they build a whole culture and education system around it."[49]

Friedman goes on: " 'In sum,' says Schleicher, 'knowledge and skills have become the global currency of 21st century economics, but there is no central bank that prints this currency. Everyone has to decide on their own how much they will print.' Sure, it's great to have oil, gas and diamonds; they can buy jobs. But they'll weaken your society in the long run unless they're used to build schools and a culture of life long learning. 'The thing that will keep you moving forward,' says Schleicher, is always 'what you bring to the table yourself.'"[49]

Columnist David Brooks is concerned that populist progressives often blame income inequality on the private economy's failure to generate jobs and on political and corporate power roadblocks. In Brooks' view the real problem is the lack of appropriate worker skills. He calls for government to expand early education, expand worker training, and provide better and more affordable community colleges, as the most effective way to improve the readiness and productivity of our workforce.[50]

Apparently the independent, nonpartisan think tank, the Council on Foreign Relations, agrees. In their bulletin "Puzzle PISA: What the Latest Tests Reveal about Global Education" they cite the following statistics from the 2012 PISA report. The United States lagged behind Canada, New Zealand, Japan, Finland, and South Korea and was equal to Poland and Iceland in reading. We were behind Luxembourg, Switzerland, Japan, Canada, South Korea. and Finland, and on a par with Ireland and Portugal in basic math skills. And in science we trailed Hungary, South Korea, New Zealand, Canada, Japan, and Finland. The document shows the U.S. failing to prepare sufficient workers to meet the needs of our life-sciences and aerospace industries as well as the needs of our State Department and intelligence agencies. Perhaps even more revealing, the CFR notes that our educational shortcomings also disqualify a significant number of our 17- to 24-yr-olds from even joining the military. Further, our shortcomings in civics training are leaving our students inadequately prepared for the duties of basic citizenship.[51]

PISA exams, that assess problem solving skills, assess some 500,000 students overall. The latest results published in 2016 show a further decline in math and essentially no improvement in science and reading over our 2012 ranking. In investigating the reasons for our poor showing, and the steps to be taken to improve, it has been shown that more spending is not necessarily the answer. Rather, the countries that excel seem to be those that hold the teaching profession in higher regard, those that focus more on the neediest students, have a higher percentage in high quality pre-school, have a culture of constant improvement, and apply rigorous standards throughout. This last requirement seems to be the only one that we have tried to address and its use has been met with a great deal of controversy and pushback. Known as The Common Core State Standards Initiative, it defines the knowledge and skills students should gain throughout their K-12 years in order to graduate high school prepared to succeed in entry-level careers, introductory academic college courses, and workforce training programs. To date Common Core has been fully adopted by 36 states and the District of Columbia, 10 other states are either making major revisions or adopting only a part of the Common Core, and four states have rejected the Common Core from the time it was introduced in 2009. And there may be more backlash coming: President Trump and his education secretary Betsy DeVos have called for a blanket repeal of the Common Core. In the light of the PISA report, this resistance to raising educational standards when student achievement in some states continues to be mediocre at best is indeed regrettable.[52]

To be fair, the problems cited above cannot all be attributed to the shortcomings of our teachers and schools. There is a bigger societal problem that must be factored in. Obviously, students from stable homes with an environment conducive to inquiring and learning, where English is the language spoken, where parents are more educated, where they involve themselves in the daily routines of their children, where they have reading material available to them and their children, do better on average whatever the curriculum standards are.[53]

In 2011 the Council on Foreign Relations sponsored an independent study of the relationship between national security and the poor performance of America's students. The task force, made up of 31 prominent education experts, national security authorities, and corporate leaders, including former Secretary of State Condoleezza Rice and Joel I. Klein, former chancellor of New York City Public Schools system, made three priority recommendations for reform:

- The Common Core standards should be adopted and expanded, with focus on subjects vital to the national security.

- Students and their parents should be given more choice in where they go to school and resources should be allocated equitably to ensure that good educational opportunities are available to all.

- A national security readiness audit should be implemented; the public should be made aware of the results and the schools and policy makers should be held accountable.[54]

What the final course of action, if any, will be remains to be seen. Regardless, we must do something more than just throw additional money at our lackluster educational system. Over the past five decades we have consistently increased the funding, and yet we continue to fall further behind.

Five Pillars of Partnership

In their book *That Used To Be Us*, Friedman and Mandelbaum identify the four challenges that will shape America's future: "how to adapt to globalization, how to adjust to the information technology (IT) revolution, how to cope with the large and soaring budget deficits stemming from the growing demand on government at every level, and how to manage a world of both rising energy consumption and rising climate threats."[55] The authors go on to say that "America built the world's most vibrant economy and democracy precisely because, in every historical turn since its founding, it has applied its own unique formula for prosperity."[56]

Friedman and Mandelbaum describe the formula as consisting "of five pillars that together constitute the country's own version of a partnership between the public and private sectors to foster economic growth. The first pillar is providing public education for more and more Americans. As technology has improved, the country has prepared people to exploit new inventions — from cotton gins, to steamships, to assembly lines, to laptops, to the Internet."[56] This first pillar is, in my mind, the key to all the rest. Without the optimal effort here, we fall further and further behind. And most assuredly, for all the reasons we have stated, our National Service program will contribute to this effort.

Friedman and Mandelbaum continue: "The second pillar is the building and continual modernization of our infrastructure."

"The third pillar involves, with a few periods of exception, keeping America's doors to immigration open so that we are constantly adding both the low-skilled but high-aspiring immigrants who keep American society energized; and the best minds in the world to enrich our universities, start new companies, and engineer new breakthroughs from medicine to manufacturing."

"The fourth pillar is government support for basic research and development, which not only increases the store of human knowledge...but also spawns new products and processes."

And "The fifth pillar is the implementation of necessary regulations on private economic activity. This includes safeguards against financial collapse and environmental destruction."[56]

These last four pillars all rely on the support of the first pillar as a strong, ever- evolving educational element.

Friedman and Mandelbaum go on to talk about what employers need today: "They are looking for workers who can think critically, who can tackle non-routine complex tasks, and who can work collaboratively with teams located in their office or globally."[57] Surely our National Service program in any of its versions will help young men and women achieve these competencies and be prepared to put them to use when they enter the work force.

James Speth takes a similar view, writing in *America the Possible*, "America can succeed only if it develops a powerful capacity to define and execute meaningful plans for dealing with complex challenges such as climate change and energy sector transformation....Planning requires, above all, competence — competence in government, in the private sector, and in citizens generally. And this competence in turn requires, above all, education and public integrity. Education is essential not just to build the skills needed in today's high-tech economy, but also to build a capacious understanding of the world in which we live."[58]

This education must include both traditional (albeit hopefully greatly improved) book learning, pre-K through high school and beyond, and the broader education in understanding and facing the challenges of the twenty-first century, much of which should come from the experiences in our National Service program.

Salvage Operation

In 2012 a group of retired military leaders calling themselves Mission: Readiness released a devastating report on the recruitment prospects of our current generation of young people. Citing Department of Defense data, they found that "75 percent of young Americans, between the ages of 17 and 24, are unable to enlist in the military today because they have failed to graduate from high school, have a criminal record or are physically unfit."[59] I think many of these young people can be salvaged and made fit for at least some aspect of our National Service program.

It's not just the military who are concerned, either. Doug Oberhelman, retiring Chairman and CEO of Caterpillar, Inc. complains, "We cannot find qualified hourly production people, and, for that matter, many technical, engineering service technicians, and even welders, and it is hurting our manufacturing base in the United States. The education system in the United States basically has failed them, and we have to retrain every person we hire." A McKinsey study determined that "American business needs to become more involved 'in developing curricula in community colleges and vocational schools, and a national jobs database would provide the basis for informed decisions about majors and training programs.'"[60] Getting fit, learning self-discipline, and acquiring a useful vocation would also help many of these unfocused youngsters find purpose and a future they could believe in.

The military teaches numerous trades and skills as part of the traditional military training and service. As we are all well aware, for every soldier on the front line, there are many support persons providing logistics, administration, and maintenance functions, most of which involve training of the type that can be put to good use once one's military service is over. Aircraft, ship, and vehicle maintenance involving machining, welding, and assembly skills are all in high demand in the private sector. So too, many IT skills associated with military service match those in the civilian job market, and could be expanded and modified as needed. Why couldn't National Service coordinate with business and labor to provide a continuing supply of trainees from the pool of National Service participants, ready to hit the ground running when they complete their tour and enter public life?

We are destined to revise our whole educational system so that those who are suited can indeed go on to a college education. Those who are not — and there are clearly many in this category — can be directed to a path preparing them for manual trades, plumbing, health care technicians, clerical workers, retail sales, food service, hair dressing, etc. that can support them and their family.. Vocational education should be directed more toward the higher end of the service sector, i.e. health and education, so that fewer members gravitate toward lower-paying, lower skills labor. (According to a McKinsey report published in 2016,[61] 79 percent of work activities are susceptible or somewhat susceptible to automation.)

That said, there are some steps that can be taken to alleviate the plight of some of the lowest paid of our workforce right now. For example, we could raise the minimum wage for all, or even for specific service sectors such as fast-food workers, who represent a very large population. Contrary to public belief, most fast food workers are not high school students working part time; rather, they are are over 20 years old, often raising a child, and the sole source of income for their families. They are also twice as likely to receive public assistance as are other working class families. Since 1938 when Franklin Roosevelt implemented a national minimum wage, periodic increases have not come close to keeping up with the cost of living. We're starting to correct this, but we can do more. Again, contrary to public opinion, there is plenty of evidence that raising the minimum wage does not have an adverse effect on the economy. Putting this additional money in the hands of these consumers apparently outweighs the loss of jobs in businesses that cannot afford the hikes[62]

We cannot go on producing poorly educated college grads, deeply in debt and incapable of gaining employment that truly requires a valid college degree. Caleb Rossiter in a column in the *Wall Street Journal* emphasized this point when he said that half the high school students in high poverty areas drop out, and the remaining who do manage to graduate perform at only fifth grade level. Only 10% of the ninth grade students that he taught in Washington, DC were even in attendance more than three days a week, and those chronically absent ignored their class work and home work.[63] I believe a general lack of discipline underlies a great deal of our society and, while it may start in the home, perhaps with a working mom and an absent dad, it is fostered in the educational scenario just described. Surely "graduates" of our National Service program will be a positive influence on this and start to swing the pendulum in the opposite direction.

We can also take a page from the European model of post-secondary education, offering some kind of formal vocational education that could be an excellent transitional step between national service and a good middle class job. In Germany, while high school graduates are much less likely to attend college than here, many more go on to vocational training. In fact, 85% of those employed in the private economy have had vocational training and have served an apprenticeship; their earnings average 92% of the average German wage.[64]. While we push college as a goal for almost everyone, the truth is that college isn't a suitable fit for many. Many college graduates are not able to find employment in the field they are trained for and, to make matters worse, they start their working career saddled with a mountain of college debt. For them, certainly, government-subsidized vocational training during and after National Service could be a better answer.

There are many callings where associate degrees and professional certifications suffice. When Siemens manufacturing was unable to find enough workers with sufficient skills to operate its new gas and steam turbine manufacturing facility in Charlotte, North Carolina, it joined with other manufacturers in the state to develop a three-year apprenticeship program leading to an associate degree and a $55,000 starting salary job.[65] Associate degrees are in many places as valuable as bachelor's degrees. In Colorado, experienced associates of applied science have virtually the same earnings as their counterparts with bachelor's degrees, and in some fields — computer engineering technologies, building construction, and nursing for example — base earnings are actually higher.[66]

Other choices available after service include joining the career military or continuing on in the humanitarian sector in a civilian capacity. Those who did decide to go to college after service would surely be better-suited to the intellectual challenges after having learned greater self-discipline and more social awareness through National Service.

The Coming Revolution in Online Education

Conservatives often tell us that government is the last organization to take on the revision of our educational system, chiefly because their bureaucratic obstacles will surely stifle any new ideas. Really! Can one honestly say that a private education system that charges $100,000 to $200,000 or more to obtain a four-year college degree is doing a fine job or is a model of efficiency? Are we comfortable that today's average graduate enters the job market owing $25,000 in tuition loans with no realistic way of paying it back in a reasonable time period? Mind you, that debt can never be pardoned. It outlives even bankruptcy.

Perhaps the one hope of restoring access to an affordable college education now lies in MOOCs, short for Massive Open Online Courses. Available through the internet, MOOCs are the modern day version of correspondence courses and distance learning, two platforms that have been providing educational supplements for more than a century. The first MOOC-like multimedia courses offered in the U.S. came along in 2008, when Stanford University experimented with "An Introduction to Artificial Intelligence." Since then MOOCs have become the fresh face of higher education, offering thousands of interactive beginner-to-advanced courses in everything from computer programming to art history and engineering on line. Any student, anywhere around the globe, with an internet connection can take these courses at a time and place of his or her choosing, for free. Produced by elite colleges and universities in the U.S. and abroad, they offer several weeks of classes including interactive video lectures and exercises delivered by experts in their fields. They are attracting hundreds of thousands of motivated students who see them as a path to gaining sophisticated skills without the cost of a degree.

There are now several MOOC consortiums, including edX, Udacity and Coursera, offering a constantly changing menu of teaching tools. Coursera is perhaps the largest. Its co-founder and chairman Andrew Ng, a professor of computer sciences at Stanford University, hoped to radically change higher education by lecturing to students all over the world, assigning and grading their homework, and awarding certificates for satisfactory completion of his courses in order to enhance their opportunities for a better job or admission to a better school. The current generation of students, already familiar with the internet, social media, smart phones and other high tech aids, are quite comfortable receiving education online.[67] Today, Coursera students who complete the work can get a "certificate" to hang on the wall by paying a few dollars, but so far the certificate is just window dressing. But when all the kinks are worked out, the bogus players have been run out of town, and the quality of the best online learning has been adequately tested in the real world of work, MOOCs may also confer "degrees" or at least college credits for successful completion.

With MOOCs as a model, government can surely design and offer its own online courses to National Service participants at minimal cost, especially if it is coordinated with the private sector retiree mentoring that I will propose. In fact this type of government and private education coordination is already underway.

Coursera, partnering with 149 institutions worldwide, now has 24 million users taking 2000 courses online or at learning hubs created with the help of the U.S. State Department. The hubs, the latest evolution in MOOC thinking, are physical locations, where students can go to get internet access to free courses supplemented by weekly in-person class discussions with local teachers or facilitators. The learning hubs permit students and instructors to engage in personal discourse as part of the learning process. Just as I propose participation by private sector retirees as instructors in the National Service program, the joint Coursera/State Department program includes non-paid Foreign Service officers and retired teachers as facilitators.

And I see another substantial benefit from these alternate higher education opportunities. Liberal schools including the Ivy League and other prestigious colleges, are justifiably being criticized for the curbs they have put on freedom of expression, particularly of controversial ideas emanating from the conservative side. The result of this liberal "intolerance" is that students are too often being shielded from ideas that offend them, that hurt their sense of self esteem, or that are contrary to the liberal core beliefs of the teaching institution. This protection has reached absurd levels, taking the form of "safe spaces", "trigger warnings", "micro-aggressions", and the stifling of guest speakers who might present ideas that offend them. Students, often without having even investigated what the speakers have to say, are allowed by college authorities to interrupt peaceful debates and shout down discussions. Like-minded faculty often lend their support to these often unruly protests. Higher education, by its very nature, has an obligation to offer open discussion of all issues, and to protect free speech, no matter how offensive to some students and faculty. Controversy and an open mind are the essence of a good education.

Our National Service program, just when we need it most, will have as one of its missions the fostering of tolerance among its inductees. In some ways, these young people will be better informed and enlightened than had they attended and paid for a four-year liberal arts college program. !

Chapter Five
Greatness — Past and Future

> *Sometimes people call me an idealist. Well, that is the way I know I am an American. America is the only idealistic nation in the world.*
>
> Woodrow Wilson, address September 8, 1919

Keep America Great

My early formative years coincided with the societal improvements of the New Deal, the military victories in World War II, the educational benefits of the GI Bill that followed, and the many improvements in the working conditions of blue collar workers. Like most American youngsters in those days, I was raised to believe in the general superiority of the United States. Not only did we see our country superior in every way to Germany, Italy, and Japan — whom we defeated — but we were also better than the Western European countries that we liberated. And we were certainly head and shoulders above the nations that remained neutral as we provided the "good" that overcame the "evil."

I'm still of that general opinion, albeit with some caveats born of maturity. I pay my respects now to the scientific, engineering, literary, and artistic achievements of societies much older than ours;

to the civility of the Swiss, to the staggeringly swift response to catastrophe of the Japanese, to the enormous sacrifices made by the Russians in lives lost — estimated at 20,000,000 — in World War II, and to the courage and steadfastness of England when faced with seemingly insurmountable odds in the early years of World War II, to mention just a few.

I've also developed reservations about U.S. superiority when it comes to our ability to lead, not only in innovation, military might, and economic might, but more significantly in our moral posture. I sometimes wonder — will it take another worldwide conflict to bring out our best, to mobilize another "greatest generation"?

I don't want to give the impression that weakness has replaced strength in every aspect of American life. In many ways we are still the greatest nation, with the organizational agility to meet large challenges when we must, just as we did with Lyndon Johnson's "Great Society" . That set of domestic programs brought us the 1964 Civil Rights Act, the 1965 Voting Rights Act, the 1965 Immigration Act, Medicare, Medicaid, the National Endowment for the Arts, the Corporation for Public Broadcasting, the Departments of Transportation and Housing and Urban Development or HUD.

America doesn't need to be made "great again" to quote Donald Trump. We need to *remain* great and improve on our shortcomings if we are to meet the huge challenges that continually face us. As we look back at the pre-election conditions in 2016 we see a five year record of job growth and lowering unemployment; our economic output is still far ahead of our closest competitors China and Japan. We have also made significant strides in reducing pollution, crime, and many forms of social discrimination. We continue to have the strongest military, and, while automation and other efficiencies are impacting some job sectors, we remain a world leader in advanced technology industries.[68]

In further examining the record of the Obama administration and the society and economy that Mr. Trump has inherited, we see 73 consecutive months of added jobs in the private sector, a total of 14.4 million new jobs, a reduction in unemployment from a high of approximately 10% when he took office in January 2009 to something under 5% when he left eight years later. During Obama's two terms our budget deficit was also significantly reduced. While we can always do better, we're headed in the right direction.[69]

One example of greatness, albeit somewhat controversial, was the 2009 American Recovery and Reinvestment Act, which made available $800 billion in stimulus funds after the economic setback of 2008. While many continue to argue that the stimulus was no better than a boondoggle, rife with inefficiencies, waste, and in some cases downright fraud perpetuated by enormous government bureaucracies, those admitted failures are only a small part of the whole story.

ProPublica investigative reporter Michael Grabell in his "Money Well Spent?"[70] details the successes and failures of many of the 20,000 funded projects. On balance, I believe that the money was well spent, producing possibly as many as two million jobs. Construction, manufacturing, education, and energy were all beneficiaries. With the checks, balances, and stumbling blocks that always attend a program of this magnitude, the Recovery and Reinvestment Act holds its own alongside the New Deal, the Marshall Plan, and the Moon Shot as an undertaking that the U.S. and only the U.S. has had the means and muscle to develop.

One of the most innovative areas in which the Recovery Act invested was clean energy development. While the package included far too many small investments designed to appease too many politicians and their constituents, and while there were some stellar failures such as Solyndra, the bankrupted Silicon Valley solar panel start-up, there were many successful projects. At minimum the seed money that went into clean energy R&D will take a long time to bear fruit, but it has made it possible for the recipients to pursue innovation which is critical to growth and survival.

Despite the huge investment involved in the stimulus package, it was not the boost the economy needed. That was not the result of poor management, but of insufficient scale. Many economists argue that the $800 billion stimulus should have been $1.2 to $1.4 trillion. But the "trillion" tag was politically impractical at the time. The Obama administration could not risk total rejection of the ARRA bill and went with what it believed would pass both Houses of Congress and be supported by the American people.

Building on the Stimulus

In my view, the Recovery Act was a good start, but one we must continue to build on. Why not take up President Obama's challenge to upgrade our nation's deteriorating infrastructure — bridges, roadways, rail lines, power grids, and so on — the total cost of which Thomas Friedman in his March 14, 2012 *New York Times* column estimated at $2 trillion. How will we do this? Specifically, by putting together a balanced partnership between public and private sectors under the current president's leadership.

Friedman quotes David Rothkopf, editor-at-large of *Foreign Policy* Magazine and an expert on global trends in energy, security, and emerging markets: " 'The thing others have most admired and tried to emulate about American capitalism is precisely what we've been ignoring: America's success over 200 years was largely due to its healthy, balanced public-private partnership — where government provided the institutions, rules, safety nets, education, research, and infrastructure to empower the private sector to innovate, invest, and take the risks that promote growth and jobs. The lesson of history, he adds, is that capitalism thrives best when you have this balance, and 'when you lose the balance, you get in trouble.'"[71]

Where we have declined, so have most other nations of the developed world, and many of the solutions are the same for all of us. In 2015 the UN endorsed some 169 international development goals for the next 15 years. That seemed like a tall order, but, as the Danish environmentalist Bjorn Lomborg wrote in *The Wall Street Journal* members could get started by doing a comprehensive cost benefit analysis, selecting a few projects that will give us significant payback both here and abroad. He cites as examples expenditures in support of free trade agreements, estimating that as much as $2,000 of value will be returned for each dollar spent on retraining and compensating displaced workers. Lomborg calculates that diversion of dollars from fossil-fuel subsidies to education and health will return $15 for every dollar spent and clean up the environment as a bonus. By closer attention to cost benefit analysis, we should be able to avoid some of the pitfalls of the Recovery Act as we invest in the future.[72]

Our military and economic might is still unchallenged globally. But it will not always be so. The anti-democratic governments of Russia, North Korea, China, and other less-free societies will continue to emphasize guns over butter, and in the short run their political strategies will succeed as their low-cost labor forces produce more and more exports, expanding economies and well-equipped military. While they will eventually pay dearly for their transgressions, they will in the short run pose real challenges to global security. However, I feel confident that the fundamental advantages that we have enjoyed throughout our history are still with us and will endure. Our vast agricultural resources more than satisfy our internal needs, and will for the foreseeable future support a great export industry. Our access to oceans on both east and west coasts, together with many sheltered deep-water ports that support shipping, enhance our foreign trade. Our network of navigable lakes and rivers gives us an enormous advantage in moving goods economically to both internal and export markets. Our natural resources are such that, unlike Japan, and many other developed economies, we are not dependent on other countries for such essentials as food, energy, chemicals and construction materials. We enjoy vast deposits of coal, natural gas, and oil. We are also hugely benefitted by having a stable northern border and trading partner in Canada, and, with some alterations necessitated by the actions of the Trump administration, we can continue to have a similarly stable southern border and trading partner. We also enjoy the advantage of having a steady stream of new workers coming to our country. Migrating from nations that lack many of our advantages, they provide us with additional labor when and where needed.

The Awesome Responsibility of Being a Superpower

Speaking before a large group in Riyadh, the capital of Saudi Arabia, at the conclusion of the First Iraq War, Khalid bin Sultan, the then Commander in Chief of Saudi Arabian forces, told his audience, "If the world is going to have one superpower, thank God it is the United States of America."[73] Reflecting on that somewhat back-handed compliment, our own Commander, General Norman Schwartzkopf, later remarked, "When I think about the nations in the past fifty years that could have emerged as the world's only superpower — Tojo's Japan, Hitler's Germany, Stalin's Russia, Mao's China — and the darkness that would have descended on this world if they had, I appreciate the wisdom of Khalid's words. Because we have emerged as the only remaining superpower, we have awesome responsibility both to ourselves as a nation and to the rest of the world."[73]

In our superpower role we have indeed saved the world on several notable occasions. But we have done this largely through

our military might. Now, however, other threats, including nuclear retaliation from any side, has changed everything. Are we
truly accounting for this in our current international policies and
preparedness?

James Speth thinks not. He has written, "The U.S. posture in the
world reflects a radical imbalance: a hugely disproportionate focus on the military and on economic issues, and tragic neglect of
some of the most serious challenges we and the world now face."[74]
Speth lists challenges for which he believes we have inadequate
preparation and no completely effective response:

- Terrorism

- Interstate rivalry, conflict, and war

- Failed and fragile nation-states

- Weapons of mass destruction and nuclear proliferation

- Genocide and mass rape

- Arms sales, legal and illegal

- Global warming and climate disruption

- Food supply and famines

- Natural disasters, floods, and droughts

- Refugees and displaced people

- Poverty and joblessness

- Drug trafficking and other transnational organized crime

and corruption

- Diseases and pandemics

- Human rights abuses and autocratic regimes

- Women's rights

73

If Speth is right, it's easy to conclude that military might alone will not resolve the next major world crisis. As the world's only superpower, the U.S. must take the lead in addressing the global social, environmental, epidemiological, and economic challenges that are here to stay. And an enlightened, well-schooled, and well-trained youth can take us there if we give them the tools and opportunity. Even as it now stands, our youth is much more attuned to the issues associated with climate change than the older generations are.

Preparing for the Future

David Gergen, adviser to four U.S. presidents, predicted that the near future was likely to be turbulent no matter what political party is in power. He still felt confident that in the long term there was cause for optimism so long as leaders can manage our deficit and spark growth. Gergen cited the following points of light:

1. Technological advances in the energy field, especially natural gas, which can make the U. S. the world leader in energy export by 2020.

2. We continue to be the leader in discovering new ways to use and to marry information technology and computer-assisted manufacturing in order to produce advanced

processes and products in the communications and health care fields.

3. Although falling behind in elementary and secondary education, by many measurements we are still the world leader in higher education.

4. Finally there are signs that both parties recognize the need to change our immigration policies in order to encourage talented foreigners to both enter the U.S. and stay in the U.S. in order to initiate and participate in new job producing ventures. [These signs are still there, the actions of President Trump not withstanding.]

Gergen also cites two promising trends: some college graduates who would have previously headed for Wall Street are now pursuing more meaningful career paths, and returning war veterans are entering the workforce with teamwork and leadership skills learned in the military.[75]

Tom Friedman expressed a similar optimism in his *New York Times* column "Who Are We?" when he identified our greatest sources of strength as "a culture of entrepreneurship", "an ethic of pluralism", and the "quality of our governing institutions", all of this in response to what he saw as the 2016 presidential hopefuls constantly "trashing" them.[76]

Our institutions are strong, though surely challenged by the rhetoric of our new President and his followers. The American dollar is unchallenged as the world currency. The FDA is a premier player and leader internationally on challenging and emerging public health issues and pharmaceuticals development. American brand names — Apple, Google, IBM, Amazon, Coca Cola, FedEx, American Express, 3-M, Boeing — . are recognized as top performers around the world. We are the world's leading energy producer. Fourteen of our universities are ranked in the global top 20. Our scholars have received over 60 percent of the Nobel prizes in medicine, science, and economics since 1970.[75]

Hollywood continues to dominate the entertainment sector. Ninety-nine percent of the world's smartphones run on two American-made operating systems, Google's Android and Apple's iOS.[77] And finally, when looking at the pluses, we are making some strides, albeit slowly, in correcting one of the most shameful black marks on this wealthy country — decades-long abandonment of the economic and social well-being of our inner cities. One sign of rebirth are rising home values in some of these areas. Another is the significant decline in violent crime in many, but not all, inner cities. Another sign is the increasingly healthy demographic mix found between the inner cities and the suburbs as some whites are moving back to older neighborhoods to take advantage of urban amenities and lower priced housing, and more middle and lower class minorities are able to move out of the inner cities in search of better jobs and schools.[78]

OK, we can all agree now that we still have a lot going for us, but are we taking full advantage of these blessings? How often do we really step forward and act like "Americans"? The simple answer is we do so only in times of extreme need. After the surprise attack on Pearl Harbor in 1941 we all pulled together, got in line to enlist, went to work in factories producing war materiel, adjusted to food shortages and black-outs, and over the next four years earned the stripes to be called the Greatest Generation.

After the Allied Forces emerged victorious in 1945, Americans were more than willing to support the rebuilding of dozens of war-devastated economies and infrastructures, not just of our allies' but our enemies' as well. We did it again after the tragedy of 9/11, offering full support to our president, at least in the initial months, despite the deep divisions that divided our people politically. We all swell with pride and feel grateful to be "an American" when our countrymen achieve technical or athletic achievements, like beating the Russians to the moon, and defeating their hockey team in the 1980 Olympics finals, the so-called "Miracle on Ice." We salute our military heroes returning from the conflicts in the middle east (unlike our shameful performance when our military heroes returned from Viet Nam). When events call for it, we can indeed pull together.

All very well, you say, but these events aren't taking place all that often. Aren't they? In actual fact, the opportunities are continuously right in front of our noses. We still have pockets of extreme poverty and misery in some inner cities and remote rural areas. We see our planet rapidly deteriorating, rain-forests destroyed, and clean water supply dwindling. In spite of our success in preventing terrorist attacks since 9/11, we know that antisocial ideologues and religious fundamentalists wanting to do us harm through acts of terror are always waiting to pounce. Here again is work to be done through National Service.

Chapter Six
The Dollars and Sense of National Service

> *Service to others is the payment you make for your space here on earth.*
>
> Mohammad Ali — World Champion boxer

How do we move this National Service program forward? For some politicians, this can be seen as somewhere between tiptoeing among landmines and going on a suicide mission. But anyone willing to step back and take a closer look will realize that our National Service program has some very real advantages for lawmakers and their constituents. Here are a few:

Financial Considerations

Thomas Ricks, whom I have cited earlier as a supporter of universal national service, points out that "the government could use this cheap labor in new ways, doing jobs that governments do in other countries but which have been deemed too expensive in this one."[11]

While his suggestions to put draftees to work at universal free day care or delivering meals to elderly shut-ins might not fly in this country, surely there is an endless need here for work details to aid the National Park service, to make improvements in our aging infrastructure, to rebuild and restore old neighborhoods, clean-up after national disasters, and undertake preservation work at historic sites. Our national forests and eroded coastal dunes also need hands-on labor. And thousands of young service people could provide much-needed assistance to our understaffed and overwhelmed health and welfare services, especially in improving living conditions for the needy.

Ricks also addresses cost. To those worried that the price of the program would run to many billions of dollars, he answers: "It would also save billions of dollars, especially if implemented broadly and imaginatively. One reason our relatively small military is hugely expensive is that all of today's volunteers are paid well: they often have spouses and children who require housing and medical care. Unmarried participant don't need such a safety net. And much of the labor currently contracted out to the private sector could be performed by 18-year-olds for much less."[11]

Ricks goes on to suggest significant savings if this cheap labor could be provided to states and cities to clean their parks or to perform custodial services at large city schools — in New York, for example.

The cost of housing all these conscripts must be factored in. Ricks proposes that this could be minimized by using former military bases where strategically located.

Let's take a look at the housing and other costs. Can we indeed afford this? I would respond "Can we afford not to do this?"

Here I offer some very rough estimates, recognizing that anything more detailed now would be pointless.

Let's first use the latest U.S. census compiled in 2010, which found approximately 9,000,000 18- and 19-year-olds, male and female, in the U.S.. Let's further assume that exemptions for physical, behavioral, and psychological reasons would bring that number down to 8,000,000, or 4,000,000 new candidates each year.

What are some available cost figures that we might use for comparison?

- The Peace Corps' annual budget of approximately $379 million supports the training, field programs, and living stipends of 7,200 volunteers (2013 data) at a cost of $52,000 per volunteer.

- The DOD 2014 military personnel budget of approximately $177 billion supports approximately 1,430,000 personnel at $123,776 per person

- The U.S. Army's base pay for an E-1 Private is currently around $18,400. Added to this is a $4,284 ($357/mo.) food allowance; a basic housing allowance in the Continental U.S. of $12,000 ($1,000/mo.), varying somewhat with the individual state; annual health care cost of $10,000 based on insurance if purchased on the open market; and tax advantages (housing, food and other allowances for the military are not subject to Federal income taxes) currently in the order of $5,000. The total, approximately $50,000 annually, should be comparable to the major variable costs for our participants.

Let's look at these individually.

First of all, government expenses for the Peace Corps should be somewhat analogous to the costs of our participants in either the military or civilian element of National Service overseas. The cost of maintaining and individual Peace Corps volunteer — $52,000 — may even be on the high side. This figure of course covers both the fixed and variable costs of the Peace Corps. The fixed cost portion is spread over a very small pool of 7200 volunteers as compared with 8,000,000 participants in the National Service program. These fixed costs, therefore, become a major portion of their total per volunteer cost. The three significant variable costs to the government of a Peace Corps volunteer are typically only $200-300/month for living allowance exclusive of housing, a minimal additional amount for the housing — which in some countries can be very primitive — and full health care coverage.

The DOD military personnel budget figure would have some bearing on the cost to support the military participants in our program, but, even here, it would be a significantly inflated comparison: the DOD's figure of $123,776 includes variable cost associated with married personnel, and it also includes fixed costs spread over the current 1,430,000 active military personnel as opposed to our National Service program's 8,000,000 participants.

I would think that the above mentioned Army figure of $50,000 should be a fairly good guideline for the variable cost of a National Service participant. This is higher than Mr. Buckley's (*Gratitude*) 1990 rough estimate which in today's dollars would be close to $30,000[79], and higher than Mr. Stone's (*5 Easy Theses*) estimate of $27,000[80]. We're all taking a rough shot, and, for purposes of its effect on the overall economy, I'll go with my figure as more like a worst case.

When we go to the National Service program, and we still maintain a career military force, we would hope that the current DOD fixed costs would cover much of the new program's fixed requirements. Other mitigating factors making the annual cost of the two-year National Service program participant significantly less costly than that of the career military person or other long-term regular service volunteer include less per-person expenditure for special weapons, special training, and deployment transportation and resettlement. There would also be no retirement benefits; the latter is a large part of the current military personnel budget.

Note also that the Congressional Budget Office estimates that savings of between $3.1 billion and $5.7 billion could be realized by employing civilians to take over some military support jobs.[81] The civilian service component of our program could well provide these employees[81]

Big Bang for the Buck

If indeed the $50,000 estimate annually per participant is in the ballpark, and 8,000,000 is a fair estimate of the number of participants, the total cost would then be on the order of $400 billion. That's approximately 2.4 percent of the current $18 trillion GDP. Currently we spend approximately 4 percent of GDP on defense in peacetime, more in wartime. At the height of the Iraq conflict, for example, it was approximately 6 percent. If we add another 2.4 percent, we would be spending approximately 6.4% of GDP in peacetime on defense and National Service. That is less than the 7-10 percent (depending on the source of the calculation) spent by Israel on their universal program.

A lot of money! Yes! But where is much of it going? For one thing, National Service expenditures pump up the economy. If globalization and automation continue to erode job opportunities, then this is a good thing. Not only will the funds cover living expenses of the 18- and 19-year-old program participants, many of whom would otherwise be unemployed and needing assistance, but the program would also stimulate ancillary jobs outside the program. Examples would be additional civilian clerical, administrative, sales, and maintenance positions to manage the military and other bases where many of the participants would be housed. Similarly, other jobs would be generated at manufacturing facilities producing supplies for the program such as uniforms, small arms for the military participants, and a variety of clerical and maintenance supplies. Such costs of the program would be returned in the form of more jobs and more money going back into the economy.

And another vitally important factor to consider: we will be redirecting some of our most vulnerable young people away from antisocial behaviors that are very costly to society and the economy. These include petty crime, drug experimentation, and at worst, the radicalization of some of our youth to terrorism, white supremacy, urban gangs, and other disruptive movements.

Since 9/11 every lethal jihadist attack has been perpetrated by home-grown terrorists most of whom had no apparent connection to foreign groups. A New York Police Department study concluded that most home-grown jihad terrorists were 18 to 35 yr. olds, relatively indistinguishable from their neighbors. Some particular personal crisis turned them in this direction. I believe that completing a tour of National Service, with its emphasis on civic education, and daily exposure to peers performing service in the name of their country, would help counter the attractions of jihad. Imam Mohamed Magid, the chief imam at the third-largest mosque in America, has successfully counseled several teens in his Virginia congregation by explaining the real nature of Islam and its spiritual teachings.[82]

David Brooks in his "How Radicals are Made" describes the frustrations and loss of self-worth of young Muslims who feel cutoff from the rest of society. They see no hope in their future, and are vulnerable to the entreaties of those radicals who decry the present, glorify the past, and promise an even more glorious future for those willing to sacrifice all, including their lives, for their ignoble cause. If our program can offer a viable alternative to these individuals before they become caught up in radicalism, if we can substitute our positive "mass movement" for their movements and turn them into loyal Americans, we will have enormous return on our investment.[83]

Now factor in the better-educated, better-motivated, more skilled end product that our program produces when compared to our current system, and it appears that we have indeed made a good investment. Our National Service will annually release thousands of more seasoned, more productive young people. Some will go on to tackle the challenges of college and advanced education before choosing their life's work; others will go directly into careers offering on-the-job training in engineering, science, communications technology, transportation, manufacturing, and health care.

It will do for our country much of what the GI Bill did for America after World War II . The education received by our veterans then improved their contribution to society and the economy, while, at the same time improving their personal incomes. The result was a vast increase in tax revenues to support our standard of living. Would not our National Service investments in human capital return comparable results ? [84]

In the end, the cost of the National Service program is a matter to be worked through by the Congressional Budget Office and other independent economists. It will then be up to the rest of us to encourage our legislators to appropriate the funds.

All of the above aside, the largest saving would undoubtedly be that of avoiding another, and another, and another unwarranted war. Surely, with every family invested in America's future, we would be less hasty in jumping into another Vietnam, Iraq, or Afghanistan, less likely to be inadequately prepared, and less burdened with incalculable costs in dollars and much more importantly, in the lives of our greatest resource, our sons and daughters.

Chapter Seven
What's Wrong With Us Politically?

> *When a man assumes a public trust, he should consider himself as public property*
>
> Thomas Jefferson, remark to Baron von Humboldt 1807

Reexamining the Way We Govern Ourselves

Concern with the present state of politics compels me to make my (our) highest priority a drastic makeover of the way we govern ourselves.

In general I favor the principles of the Republican Party: *laissez faire*, limited government, and respect for the rights of the individual. Unfortunately, our current generation of elected Republicans has shown a propensity to trample on the rights of the individual as exemplified by their bias against gays and lesbians, their complete disregard for the rights of women to control the use of their own bodies, their stand on birth control, and their incessant emphasis on religious conservatism even when it contradicts well-established science or fosters intolerance.

I understand and accept, as many in Congress do not, that our federal government cannot function unless those elected to govern us appreciate the true meaning and necessity of compromise. I believe that we must support the desires of the majority without crushing the needs of the minority. One need only hear the public pledge exacted by Conservative activist Grover Norquist from many Republican legislators to enact no new taxes regardless of circumstances, to recognize how far from bipartisan compromise we have gone. Since its rollout in 1986, Norquist's pledge has become practically required for all Republicans seeking office, and even for Democrats running in Republican districts. At latest count nearly 1,400 elected officials, from state representative to governor to U.S. Senator have signed the so-called Tax Payer Protection Plan, foreclosing on his or her ability to assess legislation on the merits. Imagine the Founding Fathers' reactions to this absurdity. Imagine going to war in today's political climate, voting to expend untold billions of dollars and not implementing taxes to pay for them. But, yes, that is the way we now do business thanks to the infamous pledge extracted from Republicans by zealot Norquist.

Those who blindly support the most ultra conservative beliefs tell the rest of us that tax increases are merely a cover for the redistribution of wealth, to ensure that all receive equality of outcome. Nothing could be further from the truth. All that the rest of us look for in our taxing philosophy is equality of opportunity. There is a big difference between that and demanding equality of outcome — a difference that the extreme political right will not acknowledge. Without an understanding of the need to compromise, including redistributing some of the wealth if need be, we will not achieve or even approach equality of opportunity. The America foreseen by our Founding Fathers will continue to decline, going the way of the failed nations and empires preceding us.

Friedman and Mandelbaum make the point succinctly in *That Used to Be Us*. "Neither of America's two major parties seems able to address in serious fashion the challenges the country confronts. Their political philosophies are worlds apart, and neither outlook is suitable for the present moment. The Democrats act as if government is the solution to all of America's difficulties; the Republicans act as if government is the cause of all of them. The Democrats behave as if virtually every program the government created in the twentieth century is perfect and cannot be changed in any way; the Republicans seek to send the country back to the nineteenth century, before any of those programs existed. Neither approach will give the country the policies it needs to succeed in the decades to come."[85]

The analysts continue, "Neither [party] has the courage to take the necessary steps to address the dangerously high budget deficits: reduce spending on the main entitlement programs (Social Security and Medicare), raise taxes, and invest in the programs on which economic success depends. And neither has the courage to reduce America's, and therefore the world's, ruinous dependence on oil by raising the price of gasoline."[85]

Now more than ever, drastic steps are necessary to right our ship of state. As we come out of the Great Recession of 2009, we have an economic scenario the likes of which we have never experienced. Wall Street investors and the stock market have weathered the storm far better than all other sectors of the economy because business has increased profits, primarily by raising efficiencies and reducing labor costs. Technology, especially in the manufacturing sector, has reduced, and will further reduce, the man hours required to produce goods and services, and the resulting negative effect on employment erodes spending power and consumption, especially among the people who once made up our very large middle class.

The reverberations are felt throughout the economy, both in terms of expanding social programs to aid the unemployed and unemployable, and in falling taxable incomes to pay for them. If we have any hope at all of avoiding further descent into a welfare state, we must rebuild our economy in such a way that it will provide the jobs and wages that will enable the majority to provide for themselves without resort to government assistance programs.

A good start, of course, is to produce a better-educated and better-trained work force. That will enable us to staff increasingly high-tech-based jobs with appropriately skilled Americans rather than outsourcing them to other nations with more versatile workforces. Our National Service program can indeed contribute to the better-education of our workforce.

Nothing has been more telling regarding the complete dysfunction of our government than the history of the so-called Grand Bargain, a term used to describe a potential agreement between President Obama and congressional leaders at the end of 2012. The sticking point was the growing national debt: whether to pay it down by increasing taxes, or to reduce the current budget by automatic, across-the-board spending cuts in government programs , a draconian practice known as "sequestration". Failure to follow one or the other political party's lead would, according to the arguments, take us over the "fiscal cliff" into a deepening recession. The Grand Bargain on debt reduction — a goal achievable only through determined bipartisan negotiations — had first emerged as a potential solution to the stalemate during Obama's first term, but no effort to find common ground was made in earnest until after the 2012 election. That's because the two political parties had become such hostages to their Left- and Right-wing ideologies that they were unwilling, even unable, to compromise for the common good of the American people.

Tom Friedman in his "Win, Lose, But No Compromise" column in *The New York Times* likened our political divide to the core sectarian Middle East divisions between Shiites and Sunnis, between Turks and Kurds, Israelis and Palestinians, or Iranians and Saudis for hegemony. Exaggeration maybe, but I would imagine that many other countries looking at our politics don't see much difference.[86]

To be sure, the concerns expressed in this chapter are for the most part based on the government's performance during the administrations of Barack Obama and his predecessor George W. Bush. It is too early to predict what will eventually come out of the current administration. However, while all of us, whether or not we voted for Donald Trump, are hoping for improvement, in the early months of his administration, there is little to cheer about.

Columnist Ross Douthat in his December 23, 2012 *New York Times* article described the situation: "Our society is divided between an ascendant center-left that's far too confident in its own rigor and righteousness, and a conservatism that's marched into an ideological cul-de-sac and is currently battering its head against the wall."

"On issue after issue, debate after debate, there is a near-unified establishment [Obama's] view of what the government should do, and then a furious right-wing reaction to this consensus that offers no real policy alternative at all."

Typical was the statement by Senate Minority Leader Mitch McConnell during President Obama's first term. McConnell asserted that the Republican Party's top goal was not to bring the country forward, not to solve our financial problems, not to create jobs, not to rebuild our infrastructure, not to become energy independent, not to solve our health care problems, not to overcome our growing social and economic inequalities, but to make Obama a one-term president and get him out of the White House! Pathetic, isn't it?

Douthat went on, "The establishment view is interventionist, corporatist, and culturally liberal. It thinks that issues like health care and climate change and immigration are best worked out through comprehensive bills drawn up by enlightened officials working hand in glove with business interests. It regards sexual liberty as sacrosanct, and other liberties — from the freedoms of churches to the rights of gun owners — as negotiable at best. It thinks that the elite should pay slightly higher taxes, and everyone else should give up guns, SUVs, and Big Gulps, and live more like, well, Manhattanites. It allows the president an entirely free hand overseas, and takes the Bush-Obama continuities in foreign policy for granted.

"The right-wing view is embittered, paranoid, and confused. It opposes anything the establishment supports, but doesn't know what it wants to do instead. (Defund government or protect Medicare? Break up the banks or deregulate them? Send more troops to Libya or don't get involved? Protect our liberties or put our schools on lockdown?) Sometimes the right's 'just say no' approach holds the establishment at bay — as on climate change and immigration, to date. But sometimes, as the House Republicans are demonstrating in the budget showdown, it makes the eventual defeat that much more sweeping.[87]

"What's missing, meanwhile, are real alternatives — not only conservative, but left-wing as well. On national security, the left has essentially disappeared, sitting on its hands while President Obama embraces powers every bit as imperial as those his predecessor claimed. On economic issues, the Occupy Wall Street movement passed on the chance to actually advance an anti-corporate agenda in favor of consciousness raising and theoretical self-gratification."[87]

Following Obama's reelection in 2012, a second round of bipartisan discussions seemed possible. John Boehner, Speaker of the

House, signaled an interest in making some increases in taxes in return for reduced spending, particularly on entitlements, but once again, political pressures from right-wing conservatives carried the day. Mr. Boehner faced losing his position as Speaker if he bargained too far, and the Senate Republican leader, Mitch McConnell, was equally unwilling to negotiate for fear of drawing a still more conservative opponent in upcoming Kentucky senatorial primary when he would seek re-election. So, the self-centered needs of these two individuals prevented them from reaching any type of compromise that would start us back on the right path to fiscal responsibility and national greatness.

Ignoring the Obvious

While all this jockeying occupied Washington month after month, other critical issues have had to be pushed aside. David Brooks described just one of them in his April 12, 2013 column in the *New York Times.* He claimed, and justifiably, that our elected officials are unwilling to devote the time, energy, and funds to address the problems of those whose lack of education puts them at a severe disadvantage.[88] Effectively shut out from upward mobility by the government's inaction, these overlooked and underserved parts of our society include mothers under 30, 53 percent of whom had their children out of wedlock; the millions of people, primarily men, dropping out of the labor force on account of discouragement; and the nearly 50 percent of college students who are unable for whatever reason to graduate from degree-granting institutions within six years.

Mr. Brooks' answer was a grand bargain in which the president trades entitlement cuts for additional discretionary spending that would benefit the less fortunate, funding more pre-K education, more scientific research, and more opportunities for living wages from jobs created by expanding and improving our decaying infrastructure. These trade-offs, Brooks thought, would not only encourage the institutions of marriage and traditional family life, but perhaps more importantly, one part of the increase in discretionary spending could go to a national service program to give our disadvantaged youth a new focus and to help open the door for them to new opportunities and a better life.[88]

Tom Friedman called out both sides for their inaction: "If either of you [President Obama and House Speaker Boehner] had been a real leader truly committed to a Grand Bargain — which you both know is what we need — you wouldn't have just walked away from your negotiations. You would have taken the issue to the country and not let up until the other guy came back to the table."[89]

A particularly unsettling example of government inaction occurred in Febrary 2016 after President Obama submitted his final budget to Congress. Even before the request was released, however, the Republican chairman of the Budget Committee announced that they had no intention of even arranging a hearing to discuss this request! It is a given that a president from one party will differ with a Congress controlled by the other, but surely nowhere is it written that they cannot even sit down and discuss it head on[90]

The list of inactions goes on and on. While we have millions of undocumented immigrants, we do nothing about immigration reform. We let our infrastructure crumble around us, but take no action to fund a program of major repair and rebuilding. Education reform, additional climate control measures and judicial reform, and prison reform are long overdue. President Obama's 2011 America Jobs Act with payroll tax cuts and a massive infrastructure bank designed to attract bipartisan support and create jobs failed in the Senate.[91]

Perhaps the most egregious example of Congress's failure to carry out its duties was their failure to hold a confirmation hearings for Justice Merrick Garland, President Obama's nomination to the Supreme Court following the death of Associate Justice Antonin Scalia in February 2016. The problem was that the confirmation of Garland would have given Democratic appointees a majority on the High Court. Republicans, led by Senate Majority Leader Mitch McConnell and Senator Chuck Grassley, Chair of the Senate Judiciary Committee, simply refused to hear the nomination. They had the full support of most of their Republican colleagues. Rather than act in accordance with the very clear mandate that the Constitution gives a sitting president to nominate candidates to fill vacancies to the very end of his term, the Republicans made specious claims about the right of "the people" to exercise their voices in the choice through the ballot box in November. This was a ridiculous argument, as the people who actually elected the serving president were being prevented from having their voice — heard three years earlier when they elected Obama to a four year term. The Republicans' strategy was, in reality, to stall any action in the hope that their candidate might win, assuring a nominee more to their liking. And, of course, it paid off. Their candidate Donald Trump did indeed win and he nominated Judge Neil Gorsuch, highly qualified, but too conservative for Senate Democrats. It was now the Democrats turn to stall, but that's all they could do. In order to protect the rights of the minority, the current custom of the Senate calls for a super majority when consenting to the appointment of the President's nominee. Unable to obtain the required 60 votes, rather than working with the President to find a more moderate candidate, the Senate exercised the aptly named "nuclear option" reducing the required affirmative votes to a 51 vote simple majority. The confirmation of Judge Gorsuch sailed through and the President took credit for one of his first 100 days greatest achievements! This is a process of changing horses in midstream that, while Constitutionally legal, we would condemn as "rigging" when done by other countries. If in the future, in order to protect the rights of the minority, we wish to avoid appointments of Supreme Court Justices representing the extremes of either party, a Constitutional amendment requiring a super majority to confirm would be in order.

Of course there are other cases of stalling tactics that contribute to the dysfunction of our government.

In June 2016 there were 83 vacancies in the federal courts nationwide held up by Senate inaction. and as a result 30 of those jurisdictions were struggling with case backlogs severe enough to be considered judicial emergencies.[92] More recently the problem has shifted over to the administration with President Trump simply ignoring the urgency to fill court and administrative vacancies. Unless and until we the people, and the elected officials of both parties, take responsibility for the national issues that matter, we will continue to slide down a path to third-world status. Still other relatively insignificant issues that have diverted attention from the real business of governing in recent years are charges against the IRS for selective targeting of Tea Party and other conservative groups seeking tax-exempt status, the repeated, meaningless votes on overturning the Affordable Healthcare Act, and the multiple, redundant investigations into the circumstances surrounding the 2012 attack on the U.S. consulate in Benghazi, Libya and attempts to hold Secretary of State Hillary Clinton culpable in the resulting death of a U.S. diplomat and several of his staff.

This last issue was raised a total of nine times by seven different congressional committees: the Senate Committee on Homeland Security and Governmental Affairs, the Senate Select Committee on Intelligence, the House Committee on Armed Services, the House Committee on Foreign Affairs, the House Permanent Select Committee on Intelligence, the House Committee on the Judiciary, and the House Committee on Oversight and Government Reform. These panels interviewed dozens of witnesses, reviewed tens of thousands of pages of documents, conducted multiple classified interviews and briefings, and held multiple public hearings, at the costs of many millions of dollars and thousands of hours of valuable time. These committees, in addition to the independent Accountability Review Board, have issued nine reports on the attacks, and none of them turned up evidence of a cover-up or gross negligence.[93]

These types of politically motivated investigations should pale in comparison to the very serious and immediate problems of the North Korean nuclear program, climate change, decaying infrastructure, problems with access to, and costs of, health care, inequality in educational standards, and the burden of interest on the national debt. Can our Congress and our Administration really afford the time to argue and investigate ad infinitum political scandals?

Why, after three years or so of arming and training Syria's rebel forces as they fight Syria's murderous totalitarian government has Congress not debated our policy there. Why, after two years of fighting the Islamic State (ISIS) in Iraq and Syria, has Congress not even voted on whether or not to authorize military intervention?[94]

Focus in Congress continues to falter. During the first week of Donald's Trump's new administration, emboldened House Republicans, meeting in secret, voted to significantly curtail the power of the Office of Congressional Ethics, an independent ethics office set up in 2008 in the aftermath of corruption scandals that sent three members of Congress to jail. The plan was fortunately rescinded and the committee's independence restored when higher ups, Democrats and the press got wind of the move. Was this really an important issue to address at the beginning of the new administration?

The Desperate Need for an Informed Electorate

Endless deliberations take place in Washington concerning raising the debt ceiling and getting our finances under control. This has been going on for some time and it's quite obvious that ideology is trumping the good of the nation. Both sides of the aisle are so afraid of antagonizing their constituencies and losing votes in the next election that they have become completely impotent.

This need for a better informed electorate has wide support by liberals, conservatives, and virtually all others who do not fit any particular label. An informed electorate would not permit their elected officials to get away with session after session of inaction. An informed electorate would, if necessary, override the dictates of those who insist on imposing for the 21st century the strictest interpretation of a constitution designed for the 18th century; and an informed electorate would demand of its leaders new amendments capable of ensuring that our government remains functional.

Here's just one idea: How about adding a small number (six or so) of Representatives-at-Large beholden to neither party, to no state, elected every two years to serve one term only. With these independents voting in the House, might we not see the current partisan log jam that contributes to so much inaction broken?

An informed electorate would also demand repeal or revision of outdated laws and regulations. Many of our laws, while initially well intended, tend to contribute to growing bureaucracies with the inherent excess administrative costs. It is estimated that administration accounts for 30% of our health care costs. Consider that Medicare and Medicaid now have 140,000 different diagnostic and treatment codes which providers must submit their claims for reimbursement; think how many hours of work must go into processing these claims! In education, half of our states have more support and administrative staff than classroom teachers.

Infrastructure projects are delayed and constantly bogged down with the regulations and costs administered by a variety of different federal and state agencies. This results in environmental and other reviews that can last many years instead of many weeks or months. Our government is great in developing new laws, but fails miserably when revisions or repeal are necessary. Here again, a Constitutional amendment addressing sunset requirements should be considered.[95]Here is one area in which Donald Trump promises to do some house cleaning. How successful he will be, given all the stakeholders that will oppose such modernization, remains to be seen.

Franklin Roosevelt was one of the greatest advocates of change, as the massive changes that were introduced under his New Deal demonstrate. FDR praised Thomas Jefferson and the Founding Fathers for anticipating the needs of the future in the ways they applied their experiences with the laws, habits and institutions of the past. President Obama, in his 2015 speech on the 50th anniversary of the Selma to Montgomery, Alabama voting rights march, expressed this same sentiment: "What greater expression of faith in the American experiment than this, what greater form of patriotism is there than the belief that America is not yet finished, that we are strong enough to be self-critical, that each successive generation can look upon our imperfections and decide that it is in our power to remake this nation to more closely align with our highest ideals?"[96]

During the debates leading up to the 2012 Republican nomination for president, Texas governor Rick Perry called Social Security a "Ponzi scheme." His comments were addressed to the younger generation, but, unfortunately (or fortunately based on his comments) surveys then showed that the "younger generation" was simply not interested in the debates. Undoubtedly, a more informed younger generation would have been. I contend that taking the younger generation temporarily away from traditional educational pursuits at the age of 18 and educating them in a different way for a couple of years before they begin conventional work or higher level schooling will result in the long run in a significantly more enlightened young voter, better able to reason and search for meaning and truth in their own personal life and in the life of society.

As the Republican nomination process came to a close in late spring of 2012, most candidates, as well as the incumbent Democratic president, finally acknowledged that the one over-riding issue was the creation of more and better jobs to lead us out of the stagnant recovery we were still in. However, not one candidate offered any significant plan to do that. During this same period, former President Bill Clinton, in his *Back to Work: Why we Need Smart Governance for a Strong Economy* presented at least eight concrete ideas with the potential to create thousands of jobs. The candidates could surely have done the same but, more likely, they were scared to go on the record with fresh thinking for fear of offending some segment of the electorate. The same fears resulted in a similar lack of new ideas from the candidates in the 2016 campaign. Of course, to be fair, Bill Clinton, when he wrote the book, was out from underneath the pressure of pleasing the electorate.

Would an educated youth trained to think more critically put up with this from their future leaders? I think not. I envision a scenario similar to that envisioned by Friedman and Mandelbaum in *That Used to be Us;* they describe "shock therapy"[97] forced upon us by outside influences or, better still, emanating from a grass-roots movement within, , namely a serious independent presidential candidate not beholden to either party's ideology.

Well, Donald Trump is hardly that "serious independent candidate" turned president, but let's call him the "populist candidate" and "populist president". And perhaps his election can serve as the "shock therapy" needed. While Donald Trump to be sure is not what Friedman and Mandelbaum had in mind, he doesn't appear to be wed to any particular ideology; his choices for cabinet secretaries and senior advisors often disagree with his stated positions. He is even known to back down occasionally when confronted with push back from his appointees.

If we look for improvement under the Trump administration, we desperately need some bi-partisan assistance from Congress, and, unfortunately, we're not off to a good start. Take, for example the Senate confirmations of cabinet positions. Is there any rational answer other than partisan politics that virtually all of the Republican Senators would approve for head of the EPA, Scott Pruitt, a climate change skeptic with a history of supporting the fossil fuel industry in their opposition to power plant emission controls that are designed to protect the environment? Is it even conceivable that virtually all of the Republican Senators really believe that Betsy DeVos, a woman passionately in favor of skirting the failing public education system rather than fixing it, should head up the Department of Education?

Looking again for improvement under the Trump administration, we must be sure to define correctly what we're trying to improve. Certainly, his election indicated that approximately half of the voters are looking for something new. How do we reconcile this expectation with the high approval ratings of the outgoing President many of whose policies are being reversed now? Perhaps Obama's high marks have more to do with his personality and character and less to do with his accomplishments.

When we look at the Obama administration's foreign policy, we find no consistent, clear-cut strategy, as many of our generals will attest. While we probably dropped the ball in Syria, especially when President Obama declared a "red line" in what the

U.S. would tolerate in regard to President Bashar al-Assad's use of chemical weapons, none of us, not the President, nor our allies, Congress, the Generals, nor the populace have come up with a solution short of permanent occupation and ownership of this ruined state. As for Iran, despite many months of negotiations, we have a nuclear agreement that appears to be the best we could achieve, short of invading and/or attempting to destroy the entire nuclear program and facilities.

So, it must not have been in a revamping of foreign policy that voters looked for a change, but in the economy. Here again, it's not so clear. Obama faced many head winds as he tried to improve the nation's economic health: a weakened global economy that constrained our export business, the reduction in government jobs brought on by Sequestration, weakening in the energy sector due to an international oil glut and reduced demand, and corporate decisions to divert their substantial cash from capital investments to buying back their own stock.[98] Despite this, Obama did oversee the reduction of unemployment from 10% in 2008 to less than 5%, maintenance of a low inflation rate, and cuts in the federal deficit by two-thirds. Also in his favor, poverty was at least no worse than it was at the start of his administration, the stock market made enormous advances, the DJIA rising from its Great Recession low of under 6,000 to 20,000 and still rising before Trump took office, and finally in 2016 even real wages and hours worked started to climb.

Two negatives that continue to dog our economy are in the number of jobless people who remain on the sidelines, not looking for work out of long-term discouragement; and the number of people who are under employed, holding half-time jobs and doing work for which they are overqualified and underpaid. Both of these metrics are up, and it is here that the desire for change stands out. For these voters both candidates elicited a degree of mistrust, but Hillary Clinton was seen as "more of the same" and

Donald Trump represented the promise of change, at least in its dysfunctional government.

In the next chapter we will see where some of the opportunities for real change lie, and how future generations made up of participants in our National Service Program will contribute.

Chapter Eight
From Tolerance to Compromise to Action

> *"Try to see it my way, only time will tell if I am right or I am wrong"*
>
> The Beatles from "We Can Work it Out"

Leaders Who Respect Can Compromise

Now let's take a look at where we are and where we might be. Remember that one of the goals of our National Service program is to create an informed educated electorate made up of a diversity of backgrounds, races, religions and ethnicities. This new generation will have developed a tolerance for different opinions, and have the reasoning tools to examine a belief, a law, or regulation, existing or proposed, from more than one side. This doesn't come from listening only to the friends or elected officials who agree with us, or by reading the editorials in only the publications that fit our political leanings, or by attending forums supported by only one side of the aisle. With so many issues being kicked down the road from one administration to the next, or perhaps even for decades, it is impossible to think that there is only one correct answer, one inherent truth, or one way forward. We must be willing to say, "Yes, you have a point" when talking with people with whom we disagree.

In doing so, we can approach difficult subjects with an expectation of negotiating. Fortunately, there are many areas where both sides are in general agreement on what should be done, their spokespeople lacking only the will to take the sometimes painful steps to reach a resolution. Later in this chapter, I list some of the areas where our leaders could make progress if they have the will to compromise. Suffice to say here, if after trying to find common ground in the middle, we still fail to arrive at agreement, we will at least have shown good will. Everyone, however grudgingly, can then move on, their self-respect intact, more than ready to engage in the next challenge.

The key to breaking through the dysfunction of our present government is to infuse our elected officials with a whole new culture of "compromise". In a country famous for self-reliance, self-confidence, and independent thinking, a certain disdain for compromise has been with us since the days of our founding fathers. It surely reached a whole new level of intransigence when House Minority Leader Mitch McConnell proclaimed shortly after Obama's election in 2008 that the Republican Party's number one priority going forward was to restrict the newly elected president to a single term. Never mind accomplishing any of the urgent legislative priorities of the nation.

Party politics is now the norm for everything. Vote the party line regardless of the merits. Issues have become so perfectly aligned with one party or the other that gridlock is the daily fare.

To be sure, there are some positive signs that Congress is starting to realize that they must do a better job of compromising with their adversaries if they are to be effective. Take the example of House Speaker Paul Ryan, addressing a bipartisan group of House interns, spoke about the negative effects that constant negativity brings to public perceptions of how their government works: "When people distrust politics, they come to distrust institutions. They lose faith in their government, and the future, too." Ryan went on to describe a better, idealized way that Congress could substitute compromise for hard line politics: "If someone has a bad idea, we tell them why our idea is better. We don't insult them into agreeing with us. We try to persuade them. We test their assumptions. And while we're at it, we test our own assumptions too." He admitted, "I'm certainly not going to stand here and tell you that I have always met this standard. There was a time when I would talk about a difference between 'makers' and 'takers' in our country, referring to people who accepted government benefits. But as I spent more time listening, and really learning the root causes of poverty, I realized I was wrong. 'Takers' wasn't how to refer to a single mom stuck in a poverty trap, just trying to take care of her family. Most people don't want to be dependent. And to label a whole group of Americans that way was wrong."[99]

OK, that's the attitude we'd like expressed by all our politicians. Now, imagine if you will, a generation or so from now, that we have all had the benefit of pre-K early education and that our secondary education has taught us to use critical thinking and analysis. Imagine as well that our first generation of National Service participants have returned to their normal lives, either continuing toward college and university degrees or joining the civilian workforce in some capacity. Having lived and learned from fellow service people of all ethnic, racial, social and economic backgrounds, this new generation of citizens will have developed greater tolerance for differences of opinion, a keen interest in current affairs, and have their own ideas on what America's social, economic and political priorities should be. They will participate in government not only by going to the ballot box when called upon, but by keeping open communications with our elected officials, reading their newsletters, listening to their speeches, and giving them feedback on issues that they feel strongly about. "A good start," you may say.

Imagine as well under this continuing scenario, many of us will have registered as independents. Whether we are independent, Republican or Democrat, we will abhor partisan obstructionism and will hold our elected officials accountable for their actions. Imagine even that the time has come to put an end to the long-running but inflexible two party system; imagine that "political" decisions are being arrived at through the efforts of more fluid, shape-shifting coalitions. Inevitably, continued democratization and splintering within our parties will require a great degree of compromise from all involved.

Utopia? Dreaming? Perhaps, but if our institutions begin to change their current *modus operandi*, we will at least be moving in the right direction, providing a glimpse of what *could* be. And maybe, just maybe, we will step out of our collective shells and start working toward "middle ground". There are, in truth, always areas of agreement to be uncovered in every dispute, always room to maneuver. Where can we start to develop meaningful answers resulting in meaningful legislation? It's easy to say that, on most major issues there is no middle ground. But I disagree. If we step out of our collective shells, if we really listen to and read the words of those whose opinions diverge greatly from ours, we will find them. Let me offer some "for instances" on areas that we could and must find compromise, right now.

Where Can We Compromise?
The Gun Control Debate Gun control represents a classic case of the failure of our elected officials to compromise, legislate and govern. Whether we like it or not, the Supreme Court has repeatedly ruled in support of the Second Amendment that declares the individual's right to bear arms. This is not just an *opinion*, capable of

settling the matter for gun rights advocates. This is a fact for all of us. The High Court, however, did not find that this right is unlimited.

Justice Antonin Scalia, writing for the majority in the District of Columbia vs. Heller case in 2008 regarding interpretation of the right to bear arms stated, "Nothing in our opinion should be taken to cast doubts on longstanding prohibitions on the possession of firearms by felons and the mentally ill, or laws forbidding the carrying of firearms in sensitive places such as schools and government buildings, or laws imposing conditions and qualifications on the commercial sale of firearms." Scalia continued, "Like most rights, the right secured by the Second Amendment is not unlimited." It is "not a right to keep and carry any weapon whatsoever in any manner whatsoever and for whatever purpose." In short, Scalia left us plenty of room to regulate gun use. So, regardless of where we stand on gun control, we must all admit that some sort of restrictions on the types and purposes of firearms are allowed, a starting point for further discussion.

Where do we start? Assault rifles? Most of us can't really even accurately define them. Regardless, automatic versions are already banned with some very limited grandfathering exceptions. Those in favor of banning semi-automatic versions ask why does anyone need these deadly weapons. Those in favor of allowing them on the other hand might make a somewhat understandable claim that they would give them an advantage over anyone breaking and entering and intending to do them or their family harm. While there is little scientific evidence to support this, it is an argument that gun control advocates cannot win.[100] Or the guns rights advocates might make another somewhat understandable claim that using semi-automatic assault rifles for target practice is a harmless challenging and enjoyable sporting activity. Again, an argument hard to refute. And, there is no compelling evidence that the federal assault weapons ban in effect from 1994 until 2004 saved any lives.[101]

Bottom line: our rate of gun homicides per population is more than five times that of the next highest advanced western nation.[102] Our nation is infatuated with guns. But there is a middle ground where progress can be found right now if we look hard enough. It is found in two places, both supported by the vast majority of Americans, and they are **universal background checks** and **gun safety**. We are making great strides in many states toward enacting universal background checks; more than 30 states currently require almost all federal firearms transactions to be recorded with the authorities and go through the FBI's National Instant Criminal Background Check System (NICS), but this accounts for only about 60 percent of sales. Federal law, however, does not require background checks on the other 40 percent which are obtained through private sale or transfer, either in-person or through internet sales.[103]

Ongoing efforts in Washington to close this very large loophole have failed repeatedly, thanks in large part to the lobbying efforts of the National Rifle Association. As recently as January 2017 the new Trump Administration has announced its intention to rescind an end-of-term Obama regulation that would prohibit the sale of guns to recipients identified as receiving disability assistance because of a disabling mental disorder and the inability to manage one's own personal affairs, claiming once again that it violates their Second Amendment rights.[104] Yet we can state with certainty that, were background checks applied to all gun sales, with no exceptions, the number of guns in the hands of those unfit to own them would surely be substantially reduced, as would the incidence of violence and murders. Granted, many individuals with confirmed terrorist leanings as well as ordinary criminals would still manage to obtain guns from illegal sources, and there will always be threats of violence, but statistics from a study by the Center for American Progress shows that gun deaths in states with weaker gun control laws, Alaska, Louisiana, and Mississippi for example, are higher than those of states with tougher laws, for example, Connecticut, Massachusetts, New Jersey and New York.[105]

The other place where consensus could be achieved is in "gun safety". Surely, everyone is in favor of "gun safety".

The term encompasses such devices as a child-proof safety lock, a loading indicator that shows if there is ammunition in the chamber, and provisions for storing guns in locked cabinets when not in use. No, again the NRA stands in the way of enacting gun safety measures, arguing that the mere availability of certain gun safety features slows down access to firepower when it is needed in an emergency, and that such mandates are just another form of interference in gun owners' lives.

Deaths from guns in the US, including suicides, homicides and accidents now total more than 30,000 annually. Over the past 30 years or so there were more deaths from guns in the U.S, than in all of the wars since our founding[106]. Traditionally, when we see similar statistics surrounding other causes of death, automobile accidents, tobacco, unsafe food and drugs, swimming pools, children's toys and so on — we respond with appropriate policies and regulations to reduce incidences. By contrast, our response to gun safety issues has been limited at best, and now the likelihood of doing anything more is remote, due primarily to pressure from the NRA.

Following the tragic shootings at a rural Connecticut school in 2012, President Obama called on gun manufacturers to do more research into "smart guns"; these firearms use radio signals or fingerprint scanners to ensure that a weapon cannot be fired by anyone but its licensed owner, and thereby avoiding accidental discharges by children and other adults. The same technology also discourages gun theft, which when one considers that some half million guns are stolen each year[107] would surely reduce shootings significantly.

With these statistics, it's almost impossible to believe that there has been a long-standing ban on CDC gun violence research reaffirmed by Congress in December 2015.[108] Why is this? Obviously, as mentioned above, lobbying by the gun industry and their mouthpiece the NRA, the totally unsubstantiated reasoning being that merely allowing safety features in guns would inevitably lead to mandating them.

Gun rights advocates tell us that design features that are designed to prevent a gun from being fired by anyone but the owner are not totally effective and, therefore, should not be required. If that is the case, then it is certainly not unreasonable for someone to object to them being required. On the other hand, if they are at all effective, then no one should argue that it is unreasonable for someone, who has a pistol in his home and wishes to minimize the chance of it being misused by a child, to be able to purchase a gun with these features. Again, there is surely room for compromise here. With a little effort by elected officials willing to stand up and support the overwhelming majority of their constituents, this could be reversed.

For more on this topic read *The Gun Debate — What Everyone Needs to know* by Philip J. Cook and Kristin A. Goss.[109] The authors, both highly respected professors in Public Policy at Duke University, have thoroughly researched the history, advocacy, and effectiveness of gun control and gun safety efforts here and abroad. There are no magic answers going forward, but if we look at the issues as a public health crisis, we can surely find a compromise that works for everyone.

The Effect of International Trade on Jobs. International trade has played an enormous role in global social and economic progress. Milestones include the 1934 Trade Agreement Act, the 1947

General Agreement on Trade and Tariffs (GATT) and the establishment of the intergovernmental World Trade Organization (WTO) in 1995. U.S. annual trade volume now exceeds $4 trillion[110], growing from 10% to 30% as a share of GDP over the past 50 years.[111] We and our global customers benefit from the technology and sophisticated high value manufacturing and agricultural products and services that we create and export when the markets of the rest of the world are open to us. Conversely we and our suppliers benefit from the lower cost commodities and less complex products that we import.

There is no doubt that trade agreements protecting some workers from having their jobs exported to low wage countries are needed. But, globalization is here to stay. Going back to an isolationist economy and building up barriers to free trade will only involve the U.S. in trade wars, increasing the prices of goods imported from China, Mexico and other low cost sources, and that will have a serious negative effect on the cost of living for everyone, but most particularly, our working class. It will also raise the cost of our production and thereby measurably reduce our export trade. And in the wake of preserving American jobs in industries where we do not necessarily excel, and where our products and services are not globally competitive, we will ultimately lose. Bear in mind that the jobs we are losing to lower wage competitors abroad represent a relatively small part of the manufacturing jobs lost. More jobs are simply being replaced by robots, computers and other technological advances, and this will only increase over time. In the words of the American business consultant Warren Bennis, "The factory of the future will have only two employees, a man and a dog. The man will be there to feed the dog. The dog will be there to keep the man from touching the equipment."[112]

So, how do we counter these oft-expressed fears? First, make sure that in any trade agreement, including a renegotiated North American Free Trade Agreement (NAFTA) or a revised

Trans-Pacific Partnership (TPP), that we are protected against foreign currency manipulation, dumping, and other practices that would leave us at a disadvantage. Then enter into the agreements, but with the proviso that short-term trade assistance protection (wage insurance and tax-payer funded training as appropriate) is included for identified groups of workers subject to being replaced as the result of certain provisions of these negotiated trade agreements. That said, in the future, with improvements in our education system as addressed in Chapter Four, we will hope that our work force is already better educated and trained for new jobs to replace jobs lost as the result of trade deals.

Liberals and conservatives, pro traders and isolationists, can surely agree on these concepts and be able to compromise the details, so that new free trade agreements can go forward. Without a TPP we are surely ceding power and prestige to the Chinese in the control of trade in the Pacific.

Welfare. Face it, we're all on welfare now! When we or our conservative legislators start talking about the free handouts that we're giving to the unemployed, or the vast numbers with low earnings who pay no income taxes, or when we complain about the amount of SNAP food stamps given out, we should look in the mirror. We all receive plenty of handouts. For example, Medicare, for which the government picks up much of the tab; the mortgage deduction; the deductions for the taxes we pay to our municipal and state governments; the lowered capital gains tax rate that favors the rich; the avoidance of taxes on overseas profits; the estate tax; the "business expense" deductions that some people get for entertaining, fine dinners out, and travel; and a myriad of other tax benefits and loopholes.

The cost of food stamps given to those with low or no income pales in comparison, and we should all be aware that most of those receiving food stamps are not shiftless bums sitting around watching TV all day. Rather, they are hard working individuals whose wages simply do not cover the basic cost of living in today's America. These are not just the opinions of one side. They are indisputable facts affirmed by reputable economic studies. If we and our elected officials start from these givens, it should be a lot easier to compromise and develop appropriate safety net legislation. A renewed investigation and implementation of the role of "workfare", in which unemployed but able adults are required to earn their public welfare benefit by performing public service jobs, would fit in nicely with a discussion of compromise

Climate Control. Legislation relating to the effects on our economy and jobs of climate control measures is another area where there is some general agreement from which a compromise could be developed. I think there finally is no doubt in most people's minds that the climate is warming up, as even the Senate confirmed in January 2016, and that there will be some serious negative effects, but perhaps some positives too. Where there is still significant disagreement is on how much of the warming is the result of man's involvement. Are we at least partially to blame? We should continue studies to get a better handle on this, but, in the meantime, let's take a look at the steps that have been proposed to counter the effects of our alleged involvement. Would these steps have any benefits aside from reducing global warming? And the answer is a resounding yes. Reducing automotive emissions, and reducing airborne pollutants from factories and fossil fuel power plants will have significant positive effects on health. Further reducing the amount of oil that we import from the middle east will give us more leverage in our dealings with our allies and adversaries there. Do these outweigh the negative effects of the alleged increased costs to the automotive industry, the loss of jobs in the coal and oil mining and exploration, and the added costs of switching to solar and wind for power generation? I would say yes. Recent indications from the automotive industry are that the costs of increasing mileage standards are not going to be as detrimental as originally anticipated. We can, as mentioned in the above discussion of trade, develop a plan to provide wage support to displaced workers in the coal mines and oil fields, and the cost of solar and wind power generation are being drastically reduced as we develop the technologies. In short, there is ample room for compromise on steps to be taken without ever addressing the role of humans in global warming.

And there is one other factor related to climate change on which all of us can agree. President Obama played the leading role in the Paris Agreement to mitigate greenhouse gas emissions signed by 194 member countries in the United Nations Framework Convention on Climate Change. If we back out of our commitment, as threatened by President Trump, regardless of the merits of the agreement, our reputation as a world leader whose word can be relied on will suffer immensely. China will continue their leadership in the development of renewable energy sources, and we will indeed be looked upon as an also ran.

Job Creation. While the Republicans cry that jobs are created by providing favorable economic conditions such as reduced corporate taxes and the elimination of excessive regulations and laws, there is plenty of solid evidence that other approaches also work. Think back to the days of the land grants made to railroads to stimulate the opening of new territories and opportunities in the West; think of the Morrill Acts that financed the building of scores of public institutions of higher learning to educate the new generations of scientific farmers, scientists and engineers needed for industrializing America. Think of the 1944 GI Bill (officially the Servicemen's Readjustment Act) that encouraged nearly eight million veterans returning from World War II to obtain a college education qualifying them for productive rewarding employment. Then consider the direct government-created jobs in building new infrastructure in the 1930s, including the Hoover Dam and the Tennessee Valley Authority that electrified a large rural area of the south. And who can forget the rapid and gargantuan build-up of the military-industrial complex beginning at the start of WWII and extending to the present. The point is that we cannot discount the government's role in creating jobs. Deregulation to create a better economic climate for job creation is fine, but don't overlook the fact that deregulation also has its downside, eliminating many office and clerical jobs, especially in health care, occupational safety, and environmental protection that manage the regulations. I'm not taking either side now, just saying that the issue is not black and white.[113]

Healthcare. Under the Obama administration, the Republicans constantly wasted time proposing the repeal of the Affordable Care Act (ACA) when they had no chance of succeeding. Then, with control in hand of the White House and both chambers of Congress, the Trump administration in its effort to undue President Obama's signature achievement made a strategic miscalculation by proposing a totally inadequate "repeal and replace" bill. This time, however, the bill was defeated not solely by the opposition party, the Democrats, but also by opposing factions within the sponsoring party, the Republicans. This was surely the ultimate example of a failure to compromise leading to an inability to govern. Admittedly, in this case it was a good thing, as the bill proposed was a toxic mix of giveaways and take-backs that would accomplish the goals of neither party nor of their constituencies. Over the preceding seven or eight years, the Republicans clearly had not done their homework. They could have picked some low hanging fruit and claimed a quick victory by correcting one or two of the universally disliked features of the ACA. Then, at the same time, they could have done a better job of defining and confirming for comparison purposes the total cost of the ACA, the total cost of replacing it with an expansion of Medicare and Medicaid and the total cost of replacing it with a new "single payer" system. Only with that information, can we hope to find areas for compromise and the eventual development of something better than the ACA.

Abortion. Is this an issue that should be politicized and governed by the state, or is it strictly a religious issue? Doesn't it depend on how we individually define life or a person? If we consider the unborn fetus having reached a certain stage a human life or a person, not a totally unreasonable definition, then it's hard to argue that taking this life is not a state issue. On the other hand, if we consider, for example, that a just conceived microscopic egg, is not a human life or a person, again, not a totally unreasonable position, then it's hard to argue that this is a state issue. Wait, don't immediately make a judgement based on your pre-conceived notion. After all, this notion is more likely than not based on the way you were brought up. Ask yourself truly, are either of the two positions I have described, positions that a reasonable rationally thinking person, someone other than you or your friends and colleagues, would not possibly take. Let's look for other areas in which to compromise.

Both sides are against abortion in principle. However, we can say that, in addition to a legal ban on abortions, with or without exceptions, there are other ways to reduce abortions. Planned Parenthood offers counseling to this end which all parties can support. Planned Parenthood offers assistance with contraception that indisputably has a positive effect on reducing abortions. Efforts to defund and close down Planned Parenthood will only increase abortions. Perhaps there is room for compromise here.

Cuba: I am amazed that, over the many years since 1962 when we imposed a trade embargo on Cuba, with the exception of Mr. Kruschev's failed attempt to install missiles, the Chinese and/or the Russians have not made more attempts to become more involved with the Cuban economy and society, and gain a foothold in our backyard. Now that President Obama has opened the door by using his executive authority to develop trade and travel, albeit limited, with Cuba, I think we should keep this in mind as we discuss and negotiate further improved relations. This concern could be the basis for compromise between those favoring, and those continuing to oppose, improved relations.

In sum, there's plenty of room here to bring our citizens and our legislators together if we are willing to seriously address both sides of the issues. It must start with listening thoughtfully and critically to the national news, preferably to newscasts that aim at objectivity and not to partisan cable news fronts; it ends with our communicating our wishes to our legislators and their doing our bidding. Avoid the temptation to vote the "party line" regardless. If you're a dedicated small government conservative, understand the difference between an "expense" and an "investment". For example, increasing funding if it leads to much needed infrastructure repair can be a win rather than only a cost or expense. Don't let anger be the basis of judgment The Republicans were so angry about President Obama's progressive agenda that they opposed some of the very same positions that they supported when the Republicans were in control a few years earlier.[114] Unfortunately, in the early days of the Trump administration, there are signs that the Democrats may play the same anger game.

Anger at Saudi Arabia for having harbored many of the terrorists who committed the attacks of 9/11 prompted a Republican Congress to enact The Justice Against Sponsors of Terrorism Act, which permitted American families who lost members in the attacks to sue Saudi rulers. Even when Obama vetoed the bill, saying that eliminating the historic notion of sovereign immunity would have the unintended consequence of jeopardizing U.S. interests, putting American service members and elected officials at risk of being tried in foreign courts, they overrode his veto and the bill stood. All very understandable, but the reciprocal has exposed us to lawsuits abroad for the many justified military and financial actions that we have taken that are considered by our enemies to be acts of terrorism.[115]

Perhaps President Obama best expressed the spirit of cooperation in his address to the 2016 graduates of Howard University:
"If you think that the only way forward is to be as uncompromis-
ing as possible, you will feel good about yourself, you will enjoy a
certain moral purity, but you're not going to get what you want, so
don't try to shut folks out. Don't try to shut them down, no matter
how much you might disagree with them."[116]

Let me close this chapter on a positive note. Congress can compromise. It can indeed be done. In December of 2015, albeit
almost three months late, Congress actually passed a budget
without a government shutdown or the threat of another national
debt default. The Democrats got much of what they wanted, i.e.
no rider attached to defund Planned Parenthood, no blocking of
the Administration's plan to require fiduciary duties of pension
managers, and no undoing of President Obama's executive orders
on immigration. The Republicans also got some concessions, i.e.
postponement of the ACA's Cadillac tax on high-cost policies
and the ACA medical device tax, legalization of the export of
US crude oil, the continuation of the Ban on CDC gun violence
studies, and enjoinment of the IRS from tampering with the tax
exemption of 501(c)(4) organizations that perform as political
action committees.[117]

Now we are in a new era, a new administration. Perhaps the ultimate compromise we should be addressing at the dawn of the
Trump administration would be the evolution of viable third,
fourth or more parties. David Brooks in his *New York Times* article "New Life in The Center" envisioned a populist-nationalist
party led by Trump, a progressive party led by Bernie Sanders
and Elizabeth Warren, and a more traditional Democratic party
best represented by Charles Schumer and Nancy Pelosi[118]. Tom
Friedman wrote a column in the *Times* aptly titled "Dump G.O.P.

For a Grand New Party" in which he described a center right party offering market-based solutions to some of the same issues that the Democrats address with their progressive solutions, i.e. climate change, gun laws, and free trade with protection for displaced workers.[119]

Let's all do our part. With the experience of our National Service program behind them, our youth will lead us in following the advice of the Dalai Lama, a world leader in promoting the benefits of bringing together people of different backgrounds. The Dalai Lama implores us to stop blaming the Congress and the parties and start addressing our own behavior to see what part, no matter how little, we can each play in making progress for our nation.[120]

Chapter Nine
Today's Mission and Tomorrow's Vision

Vision without action is a daydream. Action without vision is a nightmare.

Japanese proverb

Most individuals, most social organizations, most religious bodies, most universities and private secondary schools, and even most corporate entities have established *missions* and *visions* by which they regularly measure their effectiveness. With their mission statement they confirm to themselves and those they serve their purpose, accomplishments, and readily actionable objectives — the who, why, what and when of their daily actions. With their vision statement they disclose what goals they aim to reach and what image they would like to present in the future.

Regrettably, the United States of America does not have a clearly defined vision, understood by all its citizens. We do not know where the path to a better world lies, nor what in essence it means to be an American. We have short-term goals dictated by the party in power in Washington, and a wonderful Constitutionally protected system of checks and balances to help guide our elected officials to achieve the urgent tasks at hand when called upon to do so. However, we postpone developing our vision of the future, setting aside the more important but not-so-urgent tasks as though there will always be plenty of time and another generation to accomplish them for us.

This habit of taking the easy way, unfortunately, stifles real long-range global thinking. We concentrate on the immediate problems: campaign finance reform, gun control, abortion rights, prescription drug programs, gay rights, etc. — but we are so bogged down in partisan politics that we can't even address these properly. And in the great scheme of things, were we to take no action on them, the world would not skip a beat.

This is not to say that inaction is all right — every one of these immediate problems is important to American society and deserves our attention. But the larger share of our attention should be on long-range global issues that affect mankind and human survival: nuclear disarmament, feeding and healing the world, and saving the environment. These should all be part of a clearly elucidated mission that strives for peace, prosperity, tolerance, and truth, at home and around the world. Such goals should be used by our elected officials and by each and every one of us to measure our actions every day. The vast majority of Americans would gladly trade some of our comforts and conveniences for a feeling of pride in being part of a country that is truly the world leader.

Charles Blow said in his March 21, 2016 *New York Times* article that the road ahead requires "being for something: nobility, honor and character, righteousness, civility and togetherness. We have to decide who we are as a country, not as an opposition force but as a positive, proactive force, and use all levers of power to which we have access to bring our vision of America into reality".[121]

America's Values?

Yes, we have our Declaration of Independence, our Constitution with its Bill of Rights, our Pledge of Allegiance, and our mottos *In God We Trust* and *E Pluribus Unum* as statements of national purpose. And we have every four years the platform drafted by the winning political party as a road map of sorts, to be fleshed out in the incumbent's State of the Union addresses.

But ask your friends and neighbors. Ask a stranger. Ask a teacher, a leader of industry, your clergyman, even your senator or representative, what does America stand for? What are those basic values that set us apart from every other nation that has ever existed, exists now, or ever will exist? I contend that you will get a multitude of answers, many of them even conflicting.

It's understandable. Most of us are somewhat hazy on the basic premises underlying Thomas Jefferson's soaring words in the Declaration of Independence. Even the most conscientious among us have trouble remembering and enumerating the Articles of the Constitution and the Bill of Rights.

Do your elected representatives in Washington really support, or even remember, their party's platform in the last election, let alone remember or support what the president had to say in the State of the Union address? And as for The Pledge of Allegiance, we can't even agree on the applicability of its key phrase, "one nation under God." How about our motto "In God We Trust"? Some of us believe in God, but many do not believe in, let alone "trust," Him or Her.

So let us, for starters, propose a national vision statement that we can all rally around, drawing on the powerful messages that form the common core of our national history. Let's start by examining The Declaration of Independence and the Constitution of the United States of America.

Both documents have as their foundation what are called natural laws, a body of unchanging moral principles regarded as the basis for all human conduct, from which man-made laws and a political system must arise.

The well-known words of Jefferson's Declaration bear repeating here: "…that all Men are created equal, that they are endowed by their Creator with certain unalienable Rights, that among these are Life. Liberty, and the Pursuit of Happiness — That to secure these Rights, Governments are instituted among men, deriving their just Powers from the Consent of the Governed…."[122] Our vision statement must encapsulate the essence of these immortal words when applied to our own citizens as well as to the citizens of other nations whom we hope to influence.

The same respect must be paid to the spirit of the Constitution. The delegates who wrote the Constitution held in highest regard the same Jeffersonian principles. Those same unalienable rights are central to the purpose of the Constitution which was "to form a more perfect Union, establish Justice, insure domestic Tranquility, provide for the common defence, promote the general Welfare, and secure the Blessings of Liberty to ourselves and our Posterity…."[123] The writers envisioned a central government strong enough to ensure those rights.

Still not entirely satisfied that they had anticipated every possible eventuality in the 1789 Articles of the Constitution, Congress came back a few months later to add 10 Amendments "in order to prevent misconstruction or abuse of its powers"[125], and these were ratified in 1791. Known henceforth as the Bill of Rights, these amendments further expanded on the rights outlined in the Declaration. Some of those unalienable rights I would like to see incorporated in the values expressed or implied in a our nation's Vision Statement for the 21st Century:

- Amendment I: Freedom of religion, freedom of speech, freedom of the press, the right to assemble, and the right to petition government for redress of grievances without fear of retribution.

- Amendment IV: The right of the people to be secure in their persons, houses, papers, and effects, against unreasonable searches and seizures.

- Amendment V: No deprivation of life, liberty, or property, without due process of law, and no taking of private property for public use without just compensation.

- Amendment VI: The right to a speedy and public trial by an impartial jury in all criminal prosecutions, the right to be confronted by one's accusers as distinct from hearsay testimony, and the right to a compulsory process to obtain witnesses in one's favor and to have assistance of counsel for defense.

- Amendment VIII: No excessive bail shall be required, nor excessive fines imposed, nor cruel and unusual punishments inflicted.[124]

Two other amendments, added after the original Bill of Rights, should also be considered when drafting our national vision:

- Amendment XIII: No slavery nor involuntary servitude, except as a punishment for crime whereof the party shall have been duly tried and convicted.

- Amendments XV, XIX: The right to vote regardless of race, color, or gender.[125]

By embracing these fundamental rights and obligations in our national vision, and firmly implanting them in the minds and hearts of every young man and woman in our National Service program, we will have gone a long way toward protecting our values and ensuring our future prosperity, both moral and economic. And in this way, we will truly *become* — note that I did not say continue to be — the model to which all good citizens and nations aspire. Note also that I use the term "values," a word regularly cited by our elected officials and diplomats when we are urging others to emulate our example. Yet, lacking some clearly-stated mission or vision, I venture to say that, if you asked a dozen diplomats or elected officials to define our "values," you would not get anything like a consensus.

Some may say that these values include democracy; less often, some might include capitalism. Neither, however, is required by a society genuinely shaped and directed by the Declaration of Independence and the Constitution. Rather, what is required, what comes through loud and clear, is the concept of freedom and liberty. As Ron Paul, the noted libertarian, former congressman and Presidential contender, succinctly puts it, "Our country's founders cherished liberty, not democracy."

Exporting Freedom

George W. Bush had much to say about how best to be a world role model in his 1999 memoir, *A Charge to Keep*, written when he was still governor of Texas: "The world seeks America's leadership, looks for leadership from a country whose values are freedom and justice and equality. Ours should not be the paternalistic leadership of an arrogant big brother, but the inviting and welcome leadership of a great and noble nation. We have a collective responsibility as citizens of the greatest and freest nation in the world. America must not retreat within its borders. Our greatest export is freedom, and we have a moral obligation to champion it throughout the world."[126]

In the run-up to the 2000 presidential campaign, he cautioned "Let us not dominate others with our power....Let us have an American foreign policy that reflects American character. The modesty of true strength. The humility of true greatness. This is the strong heart of America."[127]

Bush reiterated this belief in his presidential debate with John Kerry in September 2004. "We're pursuing a strategy of freedom around the world, because I understand free nations will reject terror. Free nations will answer the hopes and aspirations of their people. Free nations will help us achieve the peace we all want."[128]

In an address earlier that same month to the United Nations General Assembly, Mr. Bush defined some of the goals that he saw in our pursuit of a strategy of freedom: "The rule of law and independent courts, a free press, political parties, and trade unions."[129]

Though freedom may have a slightly different meaning to each of us, safe to say that most of us find its elements set forth unambiguously in our Bill of Rights.

In addition to the freedoms applicable to our individual lives, there are other very important freedoms that govern the overall economic and social well-being of us collectively. Take free markets. Even the Scot moral philosopher and free market champion, Adam Smith, saw inherent limits based on equity. Writing in *The Wealth of Nations*, his magnum opus published in 1776, Smith declared, "No society can surely be flourishing and happy, of which the far greater part of the members are poor and miserable. It is but equity, besides, that they who feed, cloth, and lodge the whole body of people, should have such a share of the produce of their own labour as to be themselves tolerably well fed, cloathed and lodged." He called for "wages that cover the cost of living according to the standards of the day."[130]

Freedom is surely not a black and white issue regardless of the rhetoric of our political ideologues, and securing it to the satisfaction and benefit of all is never easy.

Many societies are generations away from democracy. Look at our failed attempts to bring real democracy to Iraq and Afghanistan. Look how all the brave promises of the Arab Spring, the democratic uprisings that originated in 2010 in Tunisia and quickly took hold in Egypt, Libya, Syria, Yemen, Bahrain, Saudi Arabia, and Jordan, have to date failed to bear fruit for any of those nations, leaving several of them worse off than before. However, this is not the end of the story. A measure of freedom is within the reach of some of these nation-states that are still under clerical and other non-democratic governments. They can still find their own evolutionary path at their own sustainable pace. Others, like Syria, are so totally in the grip of oppression — the Assad regime, the Islamic State (ISIL) — that they need outside assistance to break free. Saudi Arabia and Iran must learn to share control of the region and foster a cooperative effort that will benefit all. It is abundantly clear that we can't do it for them.

Beyond our embrace of the concepts of freedom, our mission and vision must also include those duties at home and abroad for which Americans feel responsible. They include, as described in Bush's 2006 State of the Union address, taking "the offensive by encouraging economic progress and fighting disease and spreading hope in hopeless lands. Isolation would not only tie our hands in fighting enemies, it would keep us from helping our friends in desperate need. We show compassion abroad because Americans believe in the God-given dignity and worth of a villager with HIV/AIDS or an infant with malaria or a refugee fleeing genocide or a young girl sold into slavery."[131]

And even as we pursue these admirable goals, we must also maintain as part of our mission the ability to field a strong, capable, modern military force that is trained to win, and ready when military action is in our vital national interest. George W. Bush's so-called Bush Doctrine called for pre-emptive unprovoked action by the U.S. against emerging threats — action that could include military attack, promoting regime change, and other tactics and strategies to protect our interests. This doctrine is intended to encourage our adversaries to pursue diplomacy before exposing themselves to military attack.[132]

During the ensuing Obama years we were still in the infancy of dealing with growing worldwide terror organizations and, due in part to the mixture of friends and enemies battling in Iraq and Syria, and our antipathy to both the Assad regime in Syria and the radical Islamic section of the militants opposing him, we did not develop a comprehensive diplomatic and military strategy for defeating these adversaries. While the Trump administration appears to see the urgency and dangers of an ideological war being waged by radical Islam against our western values, and is committed to defeating the Islamic State (ISIS), their initial strategy generally mimics Obama's albeit with an increase in the intensity of bombing with its inherent risk of collateral damage. Hopefully the effective strategy that President Trump has promised will eventually emerge.

When we succeed in defining our "values" and use them in the construction of national mission and vision statements, we will finally give our friends and enemies in other parts of the world a picture of who we truly are and what they can expect from us whenever challenges and crises come our way. And by having our allies and our adversaries know us better, a less vulnerable, more secure world may become a reality.

To this end our National Service program participants and veterans will not only live by these values, but will promote them to others here and abroad when called on to do so.

Chapter Ten
Toward a Better-Equipped Youth

> *I don't know what your destiny will be, but one thing I know; the only ones among you who will be really happy are those who have sought and found how to serve.*
>
> Albert Schweitzer

The most conventional track to a successful career in today's America is to graduate from high school and go on to achieve at least an undergraduate college degree. A positive indicator that greater education converts to higher income can be found in the median annual earnings statistics of college graduates ($55,000) vs. high school graduates ($34,000) vs. high school dropouts ($24,000). However, the extent to which a high school graduate is qualified to go on to higher education varies greatly in terms of social, economic, and academic preparation.

One of the many ancillary benefits to inserting a mandatory two years of National Service in every 18 year-old's life is that the participant's resulting change of pace would add maturity; for the confused and unqualified person with no clear goals, those two years of service could transform him or her into a highly motivated academic student, or high-tech trainee or apprentice.

This wiser 20-year-old, now freshly released from National Service with a collection of positive experiences and ingrained habits of hard useful work, is better able to choose the next right career move. Some will go directly into academia with a hunger for advanced studies; others will go into industrial arts apprenticeship programs; still others will take their first steps on the path leading to entrepreneurship. All will have a far better sense of their strengths and weaknesses and how to harness them to make a living.

Right now, a very large cohort of potentially great young adults is going directly from the protective environment of family and high school into sudden independence, with no preparation in mature behavior or critical thinking. Some immediately saddle themselves with mountains of college tuition debt and poor career choices. Some drift into low-skilled jobs with limited futures, or drop out of high school altogether because they feel estranged from conventional learning programs. Members of this last group foreclose on their futures and become largely unemployable in today's job market.

There is no better example of that than in Chicago where nearly 89% of the younger working-age black men, ages 16 to 19 were not employed in 2014, and where nearly half of those age 20 to 24 were neither employed nor in school. [133] There are, of course many reasons for this. According to a CNN poll, the vast majority of blacks blamed their difficulties on family breakdown, lack of motivation and/or unwillingness to work[134]

But for those choosing continued education and a college degree, in many cases, a change of pace for two years would mature the individual and transform him or her from a confused unqualified drifter to a highly motivated student thirsty for higher learning, and a wiser applicant not liable to succumb to the sales pitch of the for profits who promise a rewarding job on graduation but instead give a mountain of debt, $50,000, $100,000, or more, payable as you work behind the counter at the fast food chain or behind the bar catering to the big wigs in the financial district, or stand in line waiting for your unemployment check.

Also, when choosing continued education, they will be better qualified to embark on a particular course of study. They will have a better handle on what they hope to attain from college. For some, a high paying job, for some a mastery of a particular subject in the sciences enabling them to research and develop new products and service, for some public service, and for others simply a desire to become knowledgeable enough for a lifelong appreciation of the beauty and stimulation of literature and the arts. Those in the latter category will accept and manage any tradeoffs between their passion and employment issues while pursuing the quality of life that they seek.

And, during the two year change of pace in National Service, there are even some opportunities to get a head start on a college education. The American Council on Education compares military training with occupation requirements and then makes recommendations for course credits that are considered by more than 2300 colleges and universities.[135]

How many college graduates lament the fact that they were socially unprepared for college, not properly motivated to take advantage of the learning opportunities, and so, spent four years enjoying the party life, perhaps participating in some rather unproductive extra-curricular activities and academically just "getting by" enough to graduate. Your writer unfortunately falls into this category, i.e. lots of "gentleman's Cs" (with an occasional ungentlemanly D). How many times over the years have I dwelled on this? Surely my two-year change of pace in the Marine Corps, had it occurred prior to rather than after my college years, would have made a big difference in my academic performance and the lifelong rewards offered by my courses and professors.

My friend and Marine Corps companion Bob Donnelly is a perfect example of the benefits of national service right after high school and before embarking on higher education and/or a career. In Bob's words "When I graduated from De La Salle [high school] at 17, I realized that I wasn't ready for college and ... I decided to enlist in the Marine Corps to prove to myself that I could be one of the best.....One of my first observations in the Corps was that officers had it better than we did and they were officers because they went to college. So I decided that upon discharge I would go to college. Being a New Yorker, I went to NYU's School of Business ... I decided to major in economics to get the big picture, and minor in accounting to understand the details." After graduation Bob joined IBM, worked up their ladder for several years, and then moved on to Pfizer as a Divisional Controller. From there he went to Exxon as CFO of their Office Systems Operating Unit, and subsequently he has served in high-ranking positions at other companies seeking his expertise. I asked him to what does he attribute his success. He replied: "In a nutshell, the Marine Corps instilled in me a confidence that anything is possible..."!

And, of course, as I continue to point out throughout the book, National Service prepares the way, not only to successful careers, but more importantly to successful citizenship. I spoke recently with Jonathan Patry whose service as a Corporal in the Marine Corps from 2004 to 2008 included combat duty in Iraq in the city of Hit and in villages near Haditha. Previous generations of his family had served in the military and he in turn wished to do his part. Speaking of his experience , he said "I saw a world and purpose that was larger than I, and I gained valuable experience that taught me to persevere and push through mental and physical obstacles ....Much of my time in the Marine Corps was spent with others I did not know, and being thrust into different situations with different people was difficult. Since my environment was always changing, it was imperative that I adapt and consistently perform my duties...." Jonathan has great admiration for the leaders with whom he served and he told me that the example that they set has helped immeasurably in his personal and professional life. He is a patriotic dependable citizen now serving as a Patrolman in the Wilton, Connecticut police force, a position that his national service background undoubtedly helped him obtain.

Dropping Out/Jumping Back In

President Obama, in his 2012 State of the Union Address, called for raising the legal high school dropout age to 18 in states where it is now 16 or 17. Bob Wise, President of the Alliance for Excellent Education, agreed. While concerned with the federal government involving itself in what has long been a state matter, he saw a larger and more worrisome issue that overrides this concern. Almost a third of our students are dropping out of high school, and he called for an increased emphasis on education to combat this economic crisis.[136]

Two economists, Henry Levin and Cecilia Rouse, concurred in an op-ed piece in the January 26, 2012 *New York Times*. "In 1970, the United States had the world's highest rate of high school and college graduation. Today, according to the Organization for Economic Cooperation and Development, we've slipped to No. 21 in high school completion.... Only 7 of 10 ninth graders today will get high school diplomas."[137] Our National Service program contains a viable alternative for those who do not already have a high school diploma. After a two-year stint, graduates of the program will either have gained the necessary skills to embark on their chosen career path without a high school diploma, or, if as a result of greater maturity and exposure to the opportunities out there they still feel the need for more preparation, they will be highly motivated to complete their high school credits and receive that deferred diploma.

In Charles Blow's editorial "These Children Are Our Future," in the June 15, 2013 *New York Times*, he cited a report by the research group Child Trends. It identified as a major contributor to the unprecedentedly high drop-out rate today, the prevalence of troubled personal lives. Extrapolating from actual statistics and using a hypothetical class of 100 high school graduates as the model, Child Trends reported that "71 have experienced physical assault, 28 have been victimized sexually.... 32 have experienced some form of child mistreatment, 27 were in a physical fight, and 16 carried a weapon in the past year." The depressing tally continues: "21 percent had a sexually transmitted infection in the past year; three or four of the young women have been or are pregnant, and one has had an abortion. 39 have been bullied physically or emotionally — 16 in the past year; 29 felt 'sad and hopeless' continually for at least two weeks during the past year; 14 thought seriously about attempting suicide, and six went through with the attempt. 34 are overweight, and 22 are living in poverty (10 in deep poverty)."[138]

Blow goes on to say that "our problems would be fixable if only we could agree that the protection and healthy development of this country's children is not only a humanitarian and moral imperative, but also an economic and cultural one: today's students are tomorrow's workers."[138]

Unfortunately Americans cannot seem to bring a sense of urgency to this tragic, economically disastrous situation. As Blow points out, we are one of only three countries that have not ratified the United Nations' 1989 Convention on the Rights of the Child, the others being South Sudan and Somalia! While we may or may not have good reasons for failure to ratify, there is certainly no evidence that we as a nation have taken any steps on our own to prioritize this concern. What is sure: the numbers of troubled youths and high school drop-outs are not likely to decrease without some formal commitments to make our schools safer, without more services to intervene in dysfunctional family situations, and without effective remedial programs to assist those left behind to catch up.

Several economists over two decades have found that as the ages of legal drop-outs rise, the likelihood of staying in school until graduation improves; so too, the percentage of those going on to higher education and to stable careers also rises. With the decision to do service already made for them, might these disaffected youngsters even regard National Service as something to look forward to? Might they not see it as a positive new "adventure," something to counterbalance boredom, teen pregnancy, an unhappy home life, and a general sense that what they're learning in high school has little or no bearing on their world? Even the terrible stresses experienced in the lives of some high school students as reported by Child Trends could be mitigated when these youths enter our National Service program and are subjected to a structured, uplifting experience that enhances their feelings of self-worth. Instead of dropping out to numb their pain, I predict that many will come out of National Service highly motivated to not only complete their high school credits and receive that diploma but to reach even higher.

We have indicated that one of the goals of our National Service program is to reduce the education and skills gap — and thus the financial gap — between the more-favored and less-favored economic classes in today's society. But another possibility is that National Service will also provide some alternative to the despair and despondency that permeates the communities of the less fortunate in our society. Young women who see no hope or joy in their future are at high risk of falling back on pregnancy, childbirth, and a motherhood fraught with difficulties as their only way to express their purpose in life. Young men with no strong family foundation, an inadequate school education that prepares them for nothing, and a burning desire to belong, to be recognized, to be respected by their peers, are prime candidates for gang membership, where shootings and other criminal behaviors are the currency of self-expression. Available job opportunities for youngsters in these communities are limited at best, and those that are available pay so poorly that life beyond the poverty level is unimaginable.

Our government all too often ignores the plight of the underclass, pretends to lift the fortunes of the middle class, and devotes its best efforts to pleasing the upper class. Do we wonder why so many of the under privileged, especially the most entrepreneurial, resort to selling drugs and other illegal ventures in order to make a living? Do we wonder why suicide and violence are the only way out for many of them? Do we wonder why some go to the extreme of trading lives which they see as meaningless for the security, acceptance and even glory of radical Islamic jihad?

I contend that participation in our program will serve to overcome despair and build self-esteem. Some will find confirmation in thinking, "I have the toughness to go through boot camp just as well as, maybe even better than, those other guys with their easy lives." Or "Being a corpsman has taught me a lot about how people outside my community, even outside my country, live. Some are even worse off than I am, yet they seem satisfied; they have a positive place in their society. They do more than just survive."

For some, this kind of window on a larger world may show them a way to cut loose from their damaging and destructive past altogether. Others may use National Service as a chance to return to their communities, their friends and family, as a mentor, demonstrating a better life by example.

Building a Better American!

There has been a lot written about the lack of self-discipline and sense of responsibility within the current generation of youngsters starting in their early years. The more privileged youngsters are accustomed to having their parents spend all their free time taxiing them around from one supervised activity to another, often straining the family finances in the bargain. These children are likely to have minimal if any household chores. And they are often bribed with excessive allowances into doing the few chores they have.

Elizabeth Kolbert, in a *New Yorker* article entitled "Spoiled Rotten — Why do kids rule the roost?" makes an interesting comparison between the child-rearing habits of the Matsigenka, a tribe of about 12,000 people living in the Peruvian Amazon, and 32 middle class families in Los Angeles. When Yaniri, a 6-year-old tribal girl, accompanied a neighboring family on an overnight trip to gather the leaves to thatch their roofs, she pitched in to help without being asked. She swept the sleeping mats, stacked leaves, and fished on her own for the household's dinner; thus, she was well on her way to mastering the basic skills and sense of autonomy she will need for survival once she matures.

By contrast, Kolbert continues, "In the LA families observed, no child routinely performed household chores, without being instructed to. Often the kids had to be begged to attempt the simplest tasks; often, they still refused."[139]

Kolbert wondered how parents in other cultures went about training young people to assume adult responsibilities. In the case of the LA families, they obviously didn't. Lacking this sense of responsibility, many of these children go off to college, at a cost to the parents on the order of $200,000 or more, for an extended vacation (lasting four years if the parents are lucky, five or six if they're not). These "adultescents," as Kolbert dubs them, use the time to party, possibly partaking in "interesting" college-sponsored extracurricular activities, and doing practically anything but knuckling down and studying subjects that would make them employable — or, at the very least, better citizens. As a typical example, Kolbert mentions "Jed" who, after graduating from college, moved back into his family's apartment together with 34 boxes of vinyl LPs. Unemployed, he stayed out late, slept until noon, and wandered around the apartment in his boxer shorts.[139]

Kolbert went on to describe the experiences of Pamela Druckerman, an American raising her young daughter in France. Druckerman constantly compared her own child's terrible behavior in restaurants and parks with those of the socialized and self-controlled French children. French parents, she was told, simply refuse to cater to their children's every whim, as Americans do. They often ignore their children's requests and demands, or simply say "non," on the grounds that frustration does no harm and, in fact, may be a positive influence in their children's progress.[139]

Anthropologist and behavioral scientist Melvin Konner, another source Kolbert consulted, compares the prolonged juvenile period of *Homo sapiens* throughout history. "The farther back you look the faster kids grew up. In medieval Europe, children from seven on were initiated into adult work….Compulsory schooling, introduced in the nineteenth century, pushed back the age of maturity to sixteen or so. By the middle of the twentieth century, college graduation seemed, at least in this country, to be the new dividing line."[139] Now, who knows? Kids are simply not growing up, in many cases until well after they leave college, start a family, and suffer the hard knocks of our increasingly unforgiving society. What wasted years!

We cannot turn the clock back completely, but we can start reversing this trend. The maturing aspect of our National Service program would undoubtedly help many of these lost or searching souls get on their feet. No more excuses for those who would shirk their responsibilities. No more catering to the whims of those who lack the discipline to pitch in and do their part.

Community Involvement

With a revived sense of responsibility toward society, along with improvements in self-confidence, sense of worth, and individual productivity, these new generations are likely to return to one of the better practices of our past: community involvement. Frenchman Alexis De Tocqueville, whose astute observations on American mores in the 1830s continue to be quoted by historians, was fascinated by Americans' propensity for civic association, which he regarded as critical to making democracy work. "Americans of all ages, all stations in life, and all types of disposition, are forever forming associations....not only commercial and industrial associations....but others of a thousand different types — religious, moral, serious, futile, very general and very limited, immensely large and very minute."[140]

This instinct to join together began fading in the last quarter of the 20th century, so much so that Robert Putnam devoted an entire book to the phenomenon. In *Bowling Alone* Putnam showed that from 1970 onward we have participated less in civic associations and church membership, we socialize less both in clubs and with our neighbors, we have become less philanthropic, and even bowling leagues hold less attraction for us.[141] With this retreat to self-absorption, American society has surely lost some of its vitality.

David Brooks also wrote about how critical is the social glue that holds communities together: "We live within a golden chain, connecting self, family, village, nation and world. The bonds of that chain have to be repaired at every point, not just the local one....We Americans have a national consciousness. People who start local groups are often motivated by a dream of scaling up and changing the nation and the world. Our distemper is not only caused by local fragmentation but by national dysfunction.... That means there will have to be a bigger role for Washington.... with more radical ideas, like national service, or a national effort to seed locally run early education and infrastructure projects."[142] In the wake of the Trump election, President Obama reminded us that democracy require the "presumption of good faith in our fellow citizens....a sense of unity, a respect for our institutions, our way of life, rule of law, and a respect for each other."[143]

America's Leadership Abroad

Much has been written about the lack of leadership now provided by the United States in damping international crises and solving world problems. It's a typical refrain by the party on the outside. As I write this, Republicans charge that we're allowing Iran to develop a nuclear arsenal, that we're either doing too much or too little in combating the Islamic State (ISIL) in Syria and Iraq , and that we're letting Vladimir Putin and the Russians push us around on several fronts. And even where we do try to lead — for example, the advice of our government on how best to stimulate the stagnant European economies — we have been virtually ignored by the individual states and the European Union .

The U.S. record in Egypt and the Middle East is unspectacular.

We have failed to break the current political impasse between the Muslim Brotherhood and the military oligarchs in Egypt.

While we have struck a controversial nuclear accord with Iran, we have made no real inroads in tempering down their sworn missions to wage war against the US and erase our ally Israel from the map.

We claim as a key ally Saudi Arabia, whose monarchy supports the most puritanical and intolerant form of Islam, Wahhabism — and who uses so-called royal charity funds to support Wahhabi madrasas worldwide, training children in their extreme beliefs which run counter to those of the vast majority of other Muslims.

We have taken less than a hard line with the Palestinians. We have been unsuccessful in persuading Prime Minister Benjamin Netanyahu of Israel, the leader of our major ally in the Middle East, to back off on Jewish settlements in the occupied West Bank and to negotiate with Mahmoud Abbas to develop a roadmap for a two-state solution. We have now essentially given up on playing a role in a diplomatic resolution.

Many, if not most, foreign policy experts think that Barack Obama did a pretty good job keeping all these balls in the air and that his opponents lacked constructive alternate plans. Obama took a practical approach to Russia's incursions in eastern Ukraine. Considering the corruption in the Ukrainian government, and the pro Russian population living in the Ukraine's industrial east and in the Crimean peninsula, there was little to be gained in imposing ourselves militarily and a lot to be lost. In Syria, since we do not support either the Assad regime, nor the radical elements of the militants, establishing a sufficient military presence — "boots on the ground" — to occupy and hold made no tactical or political sense. Obama chose instead to provide air support, materiel and trainers to help the factions judged to be on the right side of the conflicts, experiencing minimal American casualties in the bargain. On the oceans, in both the Iranian Gulf and the South China Sea our warships patrol at will, so far without military conflict. For the most part, our allies support these positions. The problem is that President Obama was not able to articulate the wisdom of his positions sufficiently to sell them to his very vocal opponents, just as he was not able to articulate his many domestic victories sufficiently for the American voter to elect the candidate that would continue his legacy. Therein, I think, lies the perception by many Americans that our forty-fourth president was not a leader of the stature of FDR, JFK, or LBJ. The jury is out, of course, on the leadership qualities of his replacement.

On-the- Job Training in Leadership

Leaders are made, not born to the role, in my opinion. Being in the right place at the right time surely helps to propel some individuals to prominence; having certain charismatic qualities also helps. But the most important factors are experience gained from exposure to challenges, confidence in one's abilities to master those challenges, and just plain courage. What better environment in which our youth might get a head start on discovering and developing these qualities than in our National Service program?

The military is set up to run under a well-defined chain of command. It systematically develops squad leaders, platoon leaders, company commanders, battalion commanders, regimental commanders, and ultimately commanding generals who lead divisions and whole armies. Candidates are selected for the lowest rung in this leadership process based on perceived leadership qualities, with their superiors constantly evaluating their abilities and coaching them to do more as part of the mission. If only 10 percent of our military participants in the National Service program get to the first rung in the command chain, that's still a very large pool of talent from which to draw and develop a stream of future leaders.

Imagine some of the best squad leaders, opting to continue their service beyond the two-year mandate, going on to hone those skills in officer's training and become platoon leaders. Once discharged, they can apply these skills in whatever civilian endeavor they choose. Some will go on to careers in politics, some working their way up to high elected office. The point is that the National

Service program will be developing leaders that our society so badly needs, and sending them forth in larger numbers at an earlier age.

The same can be said of National Service candidates who choose civilian and international humanitarian aid options. These young men and women will be challenged in other equally demanding ways, and the majority of them will emerge at the end of their service as better, more mature, more capable human beings, ready to make their contributions to civic and economic life.

None of the finalists in the run-up to the 2016 elections, Hillary Clinton, Bernie Sanders, Donald Trump, Ted Cruz, Marco Rubio and John Kasich, served any time in the military. Many of us would agree that two years of military service at some point in their careers would have enhanced their leadership capabilities.[144]

Chapter Eleven
Curriculum in Life Preparation

Ask me my three priorities for government, and I tell
you: education, education and education.

Tony Blair — British Labor Party Conference October 1, 1996

In his book *How Children Succeed*, Paul Tough, a former editor of
the *New York Times Magazine*, states that "simply teaching math
and reading, the so-called cognitive skills, isn't nearly enough,
especially for children who have grown up enduring the stresses of poverty. In fact, it might not even be the most important
thing." Tough believes that "the most important thing to develop
in students are 'non-cognitive skills,'" which he summarizes as
"character."

Many of the people who have done the research or are running the
programs that Tough admires have different ways of expressing
those skills. But they are essentially character traits that are necessary to succeed not just in school but in life. Jeff Nelson, who runs
a program in a number of Chicago high schools called One Goal,
which works to improve student achievement and helps students
get into college, describes these traits as 'resilience, integrity, resourcefulness, and ambition.' Nelson calls them 'leadership skills'
and says that 'They are the linchpin of what we do.'"[145]

Tough goes on to state that "character is not something you have to learn as a small child, or are born with, but can be instilled even in teenagers who have had extraordinarily difficult lives and had no previous grounding in these traits.... Tough's book is utterly convincing that if disadvantaged students can learn the non-cognitive skills that allow them to persist in the face of difficulties, to reach for a goal even though it may be off in the distance, to strive for something, they can achieve a better life."[145]

Character traits of resilience, integrity, resourcefulness, and ambition can be worked into the educational element of our National Service program. Whether our conscripts enter without a high school diploma or are eventually college-bound, they will be much more valuable to society when they leave service and embark on a life career path.

There are three types of education taught at the secondary and university levels. First, there are the basic arts and sciences on which our traditional education programs are based. Second are the "trades," offered as an alternate at both the secondary and higher levels for those not suited to a liberal arts and sciences curriculum or for those who favor following a seamless school-to — career path much as old time apprentices prepared for work. Third is what I will refer to as a "learning-to-live" curriculum designed to prepare students to survive and even prosper in the increasingly challenging socio-economic climate of our time. This third educational element can be taught in the National Service program.

Supposedly, the Duke of Wellington credited England's victory over Napoleon's armies at the Battle of Waterloo to lessons learned "on the playing fields of Eton." Friedman and Mandelbaum echo that sentiment when they write in *That Used to be Us,* "one could argue that the stability and prosperity of the twenty-first century international order will be maintained — or lost — in the classrooms of America's public schools."[146] But if winning, not losing, is our preference, then vast improvements will be required. Part of those improvements can be achieved in the classrooms of our National Service program._

Every conscript in National Service, regardless of whether they choose the military or civilian program, will go through the military boot camp. Then, before the military enrollees move on to more advanced military training, such as infantry training, and before the civilian program enrollees go on to prepare for their specific assignment, they will all go through our "Life Preparation" educational program. This might last a month, perhaps more, depending on details of the final course curriculum. Content will be presented in book form or online, or more likely some combination, with brief supplementary lectures by volunteer mentors who provide recruits with an opportunity for discussion and deeper personal engagement. At the conclusion of each Life Prep course, a recommended reading list would be handed out with discounted prices for both paperback and electronic versions, making it relatively easy for our participants to further their education in these subjects voluntarily and on their own as they continue their two year tour and thereafter.

The Life Preparation curriculum would be structured around a few fundamentals as follows:

Civics 101

A federal report in 2011 indicated that only seven percent of eighth graders could identify all three branches of government; only 24 percent of twelfth graders were proficient in the broader concepts of civics which has been defined as recognizing the complementary roles of citizens, government, non-governmental organizations, and the private sector in building and maintaining a democratic society. Most Americans, asked to name the supreme law of the land, do not name the Constitution as their answer.[147] I would guess that no more than 50 percent of our high school graduates, or perhaps even college grads, could pass the oral test given to immigrants applying for naturalization. That test requires correct answers to six out of any ten questions taken from a list of 100 on history and civics. The poor showing of our nation's students will presumably improve somewhat when the Common Core Standards are imposed on primary and secondary school curricula. These standards, although very controversial when first proposed, and still somewhat controversial in many districts, have now been adopted by the majority of the 50 states.

Typical Common Core lesson plans will include teaching the fundamentals of our constitutional government as well as the meaning of the Declaration of Independence, the U.S. Constitution, and the Bill of Rights. These lessons would be revisited and reinforced in our National Service program's civics education.

Emphasis on civics should also lead to improved voter participation. In October 2013 the Commission on Youth Voting and Civic Knowledge released a report entitled "All Together Now: Collaboration and Innovation for Youth Engagement." The need for the study was underlined by the fact that the participation of young voters at the polls in 2012 was proportionately way below that of their elders. The report pointed out that opportunity for civic learning in the home varies greatly between wealthy and low-income households. Much of this has to do with the frequency of parent-child discussions often around the dinner table and whether parents encourage their adolescent children to express opinions and disagreements. In low-income households there is often just less family time available for talking and watching news reports on TV. Also, while teachers face some opposition from the public about what is taught in civics, researchers have found that civics education works. In recommending new and better approaches to teaching civics, the researchers suggested lowering the voting age in municipal and state elections to 17, the age when students are typically studying civics in school, and implementing new state standards that require students to read and discuss news in class. Such a change might also stimulate such conversations with parents or other adults outside of the classroom.[148]

Our National Service program's civics component should be a significant help in teaching our participants to examine some of their beliefs and prejudices more closely. I would hope that somewhere in this educational process, the students would learn to be more tolerant of the opinions of others who disagree with them, and realize that most major political issues are not all black and white. Take for example the treatment of prisoners at Guantanamo. Did the end — the swift removal of suspected terrorists from society through imprisonment — justify the means, which included suspension of the Writ of Habeas Corpus, violations of the Geneva Conventions in regard to the physical treatment of prisoners, and condemnation from our allies? Or for those arguing against the excesses of the welfare state, should the people getting food stamps despite working full time jobs be denied assistance if they are stuck in minimum wage jobs and still not earning enough to sustain their families? For those advocating right to life are we talking about all unborn fetuses, even those resulting from incest and rape? Do these same proponents also regard as sacrosanct the life of a convicted murderer on death row? How do we feel about the lives of the innocent civilians killed by our drone strikes in the wars in the middle east? Does the term "collateral damage" excuse the killings inadvert as they may be? Only if we are accustomed to learning about and respecting the opinions of others at the grass roots level will we ever be able to reach meaningful compromises at the governing levels.

An End to Political Correctness

Once we have a better handle on what constitutes appropriate civil behavior, we can put an end to the political correctness nonsense that has so captivated us for the past few decades. Today, no one can say anything about someone's personal traits or beliefs, even in jest, without fear of not only hurting someone's feelings or insulting them, but of being politically, if not legally, punished for doing so. A good example of how far this kind of super-sensitivity has gone was the political fallout occasioned by President Obama's innocent remark about Kamala Harris, the California Attorney General. Introducing her at a Democratic fundraiser, he described his friend as "brilliant… dedicated…tough," but then added that "she also happens to be, by far, the best-looking attorney general in the country".[149] Can we imagine anyone taking offense, or even recalling a comment of that nature, a few administrations ago? There would have been a few smiles and perhaps a few chuckles, probably followed by "You're not so bad for a president yourself Mr. Obama." Isn't it possible that the president's opponents had more significant issues with his governance about which to complain?

Political correctness will not be part of our civics training nor a factor in any of our other training courses beyond identifying what it is. We will "tell it like it is" regardless of how disconcerting, even offensive, some of the issues may be to particular persons or groups. Unfortunately, on the campuses of our most revered colleges and universities, where freedom of speech should be paramount, we have taken the absurd steps, in order to avoid offending any student, discomforting them or hurting their feelings, of providing "safe spaces" on campus where they can avoid social contact with those of opposing opinions. We provide "trigger warnings" on assigned literature that might include references to subjects, sexual, political, religious, etc. that might conflict with their upbringing and convictions. Some of our institutions no longer extend invitations to controversial speakers, and if they do and protests greet the announcement, they may be driven to disinvite them on the grounds that some students just can't cope. Practically anything controversial can now be construed as a micro aggression (a term most of us older graduates never heard of). I sincerely hope that under the culture and influence of the Trump administration, this approach to educating our youth will, to use a Trump phrase, "stop right now".

We must be careful, though. Political correctness can, at times be a little tricky to ascertain. I leave it to the reader to determine whether President Obama's avoidance of terms like "radical Islamist terrorism" for fear of offending the vast majority of peace loving Islamists around the world was correct. Or is Donald Trump on target when he uses "radical Islamist terrorism" any time he speaks of the threats coming from ISIS or any of the other radical groups with terrorist cells in the Middle East. They carry religious flags and shout Koranic verse when they attack, but does that really make them Islamist?

Introduction to Taxes, Health Insurance, and Retirement Benefits

Next, let's give every National Service participant a basic understanding of the hows and whys of money policies. For starters, let's take the mystery out of income taxes. The difference between effective and marginal tax rates shouldn't be confusing to the taxpayer, but it frequently is. I recall an employee refusing a raise I offered because it would put him in a higher tax bracket. I had a hard time explaining that only the raise portion would be taxed at the higher rate.

While we're at it, let's have a conversation with our participants about where our taxes go. Let's be sure they know how every citizen, rich or poor, benefits from the investments made possible through taxes, including transportation and utility networks, scientific and medical research, defense capabilities, national parks, education, regulatory agencies, social safety nets, and environmental protections. Let's also be sure they understand the rationale behind our various tax deductions — why the federal government has built into the tax code certain inducements to make us all participants in our communities: the inducement to buy a house (the mortgage deduction); to give to charitable causes we believe in (charitable deductions); to further education (the student loan deduction); and so on. Designed to incentivize social and economic growth and stability, these deductions have worked brilliantly for decades, though they may now need some updating.

What do we mean by "subsidies," "tax deductions," and "entitlements"? What are the intended purposes and effects of them on the social and economic health of our country? Are these incentives and benefits fairly distributed to and shared by the underprivileged, the middle class, the "upper one percent," by small businesses and corporate giants? Surely a little education along these lines would go a long way toward building a more enlightened electorate to combat the inequities that regularly creep into our tax code and need reform.

Our participants should also be introduced to pension, disability, and retirement concepts and how to make the right choices in health care insurance to fit their individual circumstances. They will be better and more secure citizens, more selective voters, and more likely to involve themselves in policy issues in the future if they really understand what is at stake.

Economic Theories
Since the 2008 financial crisis, economics has a new relevance for all of us. Unfortunately, in only 23 states are high schools required to offer an introduction to economic theory and in only 17 states

are students required to take an economics course.[150] Therefore, many of our high school graduates will have had little schooling in this subject. In our National Service program participants will be exposed to the basic economic theories that drive our society and others. Economist Donald Marron shows that it can be done quite simply in his brief book, *30 Second Economics* which would be excellent for the recommended reading list at the conclusion of this course on economic theories. Marron quickly runs through the essentials of such concepts as supply and demand, gross national product, socialism, property rights, and the precepts of some of the most influential thinkers in the field. It would not take long, for example, to introduce the student to the basic *laissez faire* tenets of Adam Smith's "invisible hand" and Milton Friedman's free market capitalism, or the government intervention-guided theories of John Maynard Keynes and his modern day advocate Paul Krugman. Our course could be very simple, with written material, and/or a lecture or two, presented in a form that everyone can follow and understand. Here's how I would do it:

Start by explaining that the laissez faire theorists say that suppliers work hard to sell their products or services for one reason: to make a profit. Go on to introduce the concept of a market economy by quoting from Adam Smith who said "It is not from the benevolence of the butcher, the brewer, or the baker that we expect our dinner, but from their regard to their own self-interest."[151] In order to make a profit and to satisfy their own self-interest, however, they must provide what the market wants. Therefore, in Adam Smith's market economy, everyone benefits, both producers and buyers. When both parties are free to choose what they sell and what they buy, the "invisible hand" of competition guides the market so that the personal initiative of, and indeed the greed of, the suppliers combine to produce an overall collective gain.[152] There is no government interference giving us a handout. As Milton Friedman so eloquently stated it, "There's no such thing as 'a free lunch.' If the government spends a dollar, that dollar has to come from producers and workers in the private economy. There is no magical 'multiplier effect' by taking from productive Peter and giving to unproductive Paul."[153]

I would also point out Milton Friedman's belief that "'Higher taxes never reduce the deficit. Government spends whatever they take in and then whatever they can get away with.'"[153] , and his claim that in order to make America more prosperous, we should do three things: "'promote free trade, school choice for all children, and cut government spending.'"[153]

Then I would give the opposing theory with a statement to the effect that countering the laissez faire argument, there is the theory of the government acting as a visible hand (or "handout," some detractors would say), espoused by Keynes and Krugman.They argue that even in a sound growing ordered economy, there will be times when unanticipated internal or external forces temporarily slow down, halt, or even reverse this pattern of growth. And it is at these times that government must intervene to help right the ship.[154] Accordingly, in recessionary times the government should spend on job- producing programs and projects in order to stimulate growth; conversely, when the economy is expanding the government should step back, spend less, and save for the future.[155]

The written-lecture handout could be something as simple as the above three paragraphs. A second lecture(s) might be organized around a brief discussion of our place in the global economy, focusing on the pros and cons of trade agreements and the role of imports and exports in our domestic economy, and perhaps a discussion of the legitimate assigned fiscal responsibilities of the Federal government, the states, and the municipalities.

With this kind of introduction to economic theory, our participants would get just enough to understand the broad concepts;

for some of them, it will serve to whet their appetites to learn more, aided by the recommended reading list handed out at the conclusion of the course.

Personal Money Matters

An introduction to personal finances would also be invaluable to National Service participants. For a workable model, I suggest the curriculum designers turn to Champlain College in Vermont. The college has developed the Center for Financial Literacy with a unique curriculum for students, teachers, and, in fact, all adults across Vermont. The Center's stated goal is to increase "knowledge of money matters [so that] college students graduate with the skills to make sound decisions about spending, credit and investments, and help adults navigate difficult financial situations like buying a home and saving for retirement."[156]

John Pelletier, Director of Champlain's Center, explains that "The Great Recession demonstrated that our citizens struggle when making complex financial decisions that are critical to their well-being. Some of our economic problems were created by bad actors, focused on personal gain, but so many others were created by good people making poorly-informed personal financial decisions."[159] Pelletier, who is often consulted for his expertise in this field, notes that "we would not allow a young person to get in the driver's seat of a car without requiring driver's education, and yet we allow our citizens to enter the complex financial world without any related education. An uneducated individual armed with a credit card, a student loan, and access to a mortgage can be nearly as dangerous to themselves and their community as a person with no training who is given a car to drive."[157]

Champlain College's plan includes courses on budgeting and goal-setting, understanding credit, sound investing, understanding employee benefits, repaying student loans, and buying the first car. And, in addition to spreading their programs throughout Vermont, the Center is also advocating for similar educational opportunities at other local and state levels, as well as the national level. Other states, colleges, and institutions are also exploring ways to improve financial literacy. Bank of America in partnership with Khan Academy has developed a free on-line education course, Better Money Habits ®, addressing payroll deductions, taxes, saving, etc.[158] However, as yet, a huge gap in financial literacy still remains, particularly among the disadvantaged.

Perhaps the most basic element of personal finances needed is in decision-making. How much income do I need to accomplish my goals? The typical answer would be rather surprising to most. For example, a USA Today report in 2014 determined that it required an income of over $130,000 for a family of four to afford a middle class life style that includes home ownership, two cars, adequate health insurance, college education for two children, an annual family vacation, and adequate retirement planning.[159] The recession of 2009 was brought about in great part by the bursting of the housing bubble, revealing the woeful ignorance of so many new home buyers about the obligations and consequences of the mortgage documents they signed.

Friedman and Mandelbaum wrote about it in *That Used to be Us*. "High-risk home buyers ... were sometimes actually encouraged to lie about their incomes — or lack of them. The broker told the family assuming the mortgage that ... if they couldn't meet the monthly payments when they started kicking in, no problem. Just walk away from the property — 'you'll be gone — or sell it for a profit because, as we all 'knew' at the time, housing prices would keep going up forever. They would never go down."[160] Really?

The lessons to be taught and learned in a course on financial literacy could easily be included in the National Service education curriculum. Had such been done in our schools in the past, how many foreclosures, how much destruction of the housing market, how much emotional pain and suffering, could have been avoided?

Lessons in International Understanding

Everyone should have a basic grasp of the major foreign policy issues of the time — for example, each of us needs to understand something of our involvement in the politics and conflicts in the Middle East and the real cost of their oil when we factor in the wars and our unwavering support of Israel. It is particularly important for our National Service participants to understand our major foreign policy issues, because they could well find themselves physically involved in them, either as part of our military force, or as humanitarian corpsmen serving in these areas. Similarly, National Service personnel need some knowledge of the foreign defense treaties we have entered into, and of the depth of our commitments when the countries with which we have these treaties are threatened or invaded.

What is the difference between our obligations to NATO nations and Japan, and our obligations to Afghanistan and Ukraine, for example? When, according to our foreign and military policies, are "boots on the ground" justified? Under what circumstances should we deploy drone attacks? What are the legal and ethical differences between the treatment of prisoners captured from the military forces of a recognized state and those captured from non-state-sponsored insurgent groups like Al Qaeda and the newly emergent ISIS?

The foreign policy curriculum could include a very basic discussion of the cultural differences between the secular and religious states of the world, the developed and non-developed, the poor and the wealthy, and the Sunnis and Shiites within the Muslim world. Why do Americans barely react, when some angry foreign activists burn our flag, while the people of some other nations respond to almost any disrespect of their cultural icons, real or perceived, with violence in the streets, suicide bombings, and civilian beheadings? Why are we often so unsuccessful in negotiating with their leaders? Well, quite possibly, it is simply because we fail to recognize that the fundamental beliefs that drive their priorities and ours are different.

We have so much going for us — so much freedom of choice, so much confidence in the rightness of our system of government — that we fail to recognize how constrained others' lives are. The burning of our flag or the anti-American raving of some fanatic Muslim cleric, is not as demanding of our attention as who wins the Super Bowl, what restaurant we'll visit tonight, what crime story has captured the news. How can we relate to a foreign culture in which the common man can never afford to attend lavish sporting events, knows no religious freedom, and has virtually all his beliefs and behaviors prescribed by custom? For this isolated individual, any offense against his or her country's sanctity and traditions, including the burning of the Koran or the ridiculing of some *ayatollah* by people in some far-off land, becomes a major incident.

In recent years we have experienced a troubling phenomenon among the Afghan troops who are supposed to be our allies. Repeatedly, one or two of them break ranks during a joint mission to turn on us, wounding or killing American "comrades" in their company. The attacks are made most often by Afghans from isolated rural areas, where their entire life experience up to the time they become soldiers is of their villages' religious and social codes, scarcely modified over the centuries. Though the rogue soldiers are often taken for Taliban fighters, Afghan advisers insist the men are driven by personal anger and the perception that their country's sanctity is disrespected by the free-wheeling Americans. In this way their acts are demonstrations of respect for their beliefs, not of political insurgency. While we should in no way excuse or condone these actions, nor accept any blame for them, the National Service program's educational curriculum could sensitize our young people to the exceptional part played by religious beliefs in orthodox Muslim societies, the better to avoid behaviors and remarks seen as disrespectful.

Current Affairs

Perhaps it would be a good idea for our service participants to hear from "the experts", on both sides where applicable, of each of the major current issues of the times. For example, were the program in place now, the issues covered might include the case for and against a single payer universal health care system, the major components of the Federal budget, gun control/safety as previously mentioned, campaign financing, and all the other issues addressed in Chapter 9 when we discussed opportunities for political compromise.

Immigration

Our country, more than any other on the globe was built in great part by immigrants and continues to benefit by a constant flow of immigrants, skilled and unskilled. Many of those serving in our National Service program will be immigrants themselves or from immigrant parents. During the 2016 presidential election campaign and the early months of the Trump administration, the role of immigration in our progress, is being examined more closely than ever in the past. I hope the country will eventually unite behind a policy that does not bar immigrants based on their Islamic religion and/or their origin from a country that provides haven for terrorists. Hopefully we will examine and, if necessary, improve our vetting process to the satisfaction of all, bearing in mind, however, that the existing process is already very extensive. A course in our program explaining all of this, if properly developed, should foster improved relations and good will among the participants by clearly describing the benefits of a larger workforce to the sustained growth of our economy, the addition of highly educated engineers, scientists and physicians to our society and economy, and the tradition and values associated with aiding political refugees and those escaping economic misery.

Media Literacy

All of our participants, at least after their boot camp indoctrination, will undoubtedly have in their possession at virtually all times smart phones and/or other news gathering instruments. Many, if not most, of these youngsters will be used to getting all their news in this fashion. Many, if not most, will probably not have been reading a daily newspaper or the online versions. All of their news will typically come from Facebook, Twitter and other social media, and much of it will fall into the category of "fake news". This has become particularly prevalent during the final year of the Obama administration and during the present administration where the President, Donald Trump himself, is an avid user of Twitter. Much of the news distributed in this fashion is impulsive and backed up by little if any investigative reporting. Much of it is in fact "fake" and offered merely to elicit a specific reaction, typically a reaction supporting the rantings of the author, though there is also a fake news industry that is simply out to make money based on its advertising rates and the number of "hits" its shock news stories drive. Trump's advisor used the term "alternate facts" to describe the falsehoods emanating from their office. This would be amusing if it were not that they deem the practice of spreading "alternate facts" as an acceptable form of communication.

Here are some particularly egregious examples. The year 2015 was the hottest then on record. Then 2016 set a new record for the hottest year during which the month of July was the hottest month on record. Now setting aside whether or not these temperatures were caused by human activities and carbon emissions, 45% of Republicans, according to a Gallup poll, simply don't believe these temperature facts .[161] It would appear that they have been brainwashed by social media, and they believe only the side of social media that supports their position. However, I would have to believe that there are plenty of other social media postings supporting the correct temperature facts.

Unfortunately, many of us no longer respect the word of the experts. Not only would we rather take the word of a random posting on Facebook than that of the scientific community when considering the effects of climate change, we question overwhelming evidence and the opinions and advice of the medical profession concerning the safety of measles vaccine.

A false posting on Facebook went viral claiming that the Pope had endorsed Donald Trump, along with a statement that Ireland was taking in from the US refugees opposed to Trump.

Then, as we all unfortunately found out, a man who read a fake news story about Hillary Clinton and John Podesta running a child sex ring in a Washington DC pizza restaurant went there and opened fire with an assault rifle.

A course on how to separate fact from fiction would offer immeasurable benefits. The underlying theme of the course would be the absolute necessity of examining both sides of an issue before formulating an opinion. Read the opinions and editorials from both the conservative and liberal city or area newspapers. Don't fall into the trap of "confirmation bias", i.e. reading only the side that typically corresponds with your ideology. Keep an open mind.

Other Life Preparation Courses

The National Service program could also educate our young participants on subjects as diverse as health and diet issues and the role of labor unions in our economy and society. Some basic tutoring in civilized behavior — what used to be called "manners" and getting along with your neighbors — would be advisable, too.

The sad fact is that we are becoming a nation of boors. Imagine the enormous toll taken on human capital and the detriment to society occasioned by the unruly behavior and lax discipline in our schools. I believe this is the main underlying cause of the advocacy for charter schools and the promotion of school vouchers. This can only contribute in the long run to the further deterioration of the public school system by diverting public funding to new, often church-based, private schools. Then again, don't just say that civilized behavior is the sole responsibility of parents and grade school teachers; if so, they're not doing a very good job of it. The military, on the other hand, sets an excellent example for its recruits and enforces it, and this can be copied in National Service training.

Military courtesy is one of the defining features of the professional force. These courtesies form a strict and sometimes elaborate code of conduct, derived from courtesies once practiced in everyday life. They are intended to reinforce discipline and to conform with the chain of command, one more way in which soldiers are instructed to treat their superiors and vice versa. Military courtesies include proper forms of address and when and where to salute, as well as proper wear of military uniform and head gear, and the rules of behavior relating to particular ceremonies. The rules are made clear through strict and consistent enforcement.

If training in courtesy, comportment and dress fits in with the military experience, it should fit in with our National Service program. Look around. In social gatherings who is the one with the shiny shoes? Chances are pretty good that it's a Marine (there is no such thing as an ex- Marine). Who always uncovers (takes his hat off) entering a home or a restaurant? Chances are it's an ex-serviceman.

Not everyone will agree on what constitutes proper behavior, and, to be sure, what constituted proper courtesy, comportment, and dress 50 or 100 years ago might not always be suitable in today's social environment. Regardless, while not everyone will make the current preferred practices, whatever they are, a permanent part of their social behavior, the training can't hurt and for some it will become ingrained practice.

We all have some "pet peeves" regarding the uncaring attitude of some of our citizenry, for example the shopping cart left in the middle of a grocery store parking space, beer cans and fast food trash discarded along our country roads, or the purposely unmuffled noise of a hot rod cruising our streets. This disrespect for others has magnified significantly over the past decades. There's a role to be played here by our Life Preparation curriculum. Perhaps we can help reverse this trend.

Lastly, given that creativity and innovation are the drivers of our future, how about teaching our young participants some basic lessons in "how to make money"? Steve Mariotti knows something about this. He founded the Network for Teaching Entrepreneurship, a nonprofit organization "that helps young people from low-income communities unlock their potential for entrepreneurial creativity by teaching them to start their own businesses."[162] Bill Gross has also explored this kind of educational opportunity for young people. Gross is the founder of IdeaLab, "an innovation laboratory that supports 'groundbreaking companies whose products and services change the way people think, live and work.'"[163] Gross claims that "the biggest barrier to creativity... is 'lack of self-confidence.'"[164] Our National Service program through both its service function and educational element will help all participants boost their confidence.

The educational curricula described in this chapter could be provided gratis by higher education organizations in exchange for expanded tax forgiveness if possible, or other quid pro quo. Or it could be provided by retired business and academic leaders, a new branch of the existing Senior Corps, who would receive modest stipends for their work.

All these ideas are fine in the abstract, you say, but won't they be carried out at the cost of a huge political boondoggle? How do we certify the instructors? How do we avoid the liberal bias of which our finest higher education institutions are accused? How do we avoid the Right or Left bias of the party in control when developing the regulations and appointing those in charge of the curriculum? As usual, there are no easy answers. Hard-fought arguments will ensue, but, as with most other social issue challenges, eventually we can get it right.

Summer reading lists still exist in our better school systems, and lengthy course-related reading assignments are common at our colleges and universities. With our program, each course would end with a recommended reading list. Follow- through would be voluntary, but I would guess that a good percentage of our students would take the challenge, if not during their two-year service stint, then at some later stage of life. These books could be the beginning of a new 21st century common core of "classic" literature, serving much the same purpose today as reading the Greek and Roman philosophers did for our forebears.

Granted there will be among our universal participants a modest number who are already thoroughly versed in most if not all of these basics. They would have two alternatives to the standard education element, either to move directly into their national military, national civilian, or international humanitarian service roles, or to take an advanced series of electives and compulsory courses — probably, but not necessarily, in these same subjects.

Another alternative for some who qualify might be a series of remedial courses in math, reading and writing for example, for those planning to go right into college after their service tour but knowing or having been advised that they are among the large group of college bounds who are not equipped in these basics

In sum, I contend that a National Service program will help im-measurably in getting all our 18- and 19-year-olds off to a better start in adult life, whether they go on to college, a trade school, or directly into the workplace. Not only will the program further the self-worth of our youth, but, equally important, it will further their marketability. We will have helped immeasurably to over-come the complaint that business has these days that too many of our young people are ill-prepared to handle the technical chal-lenges of the available jobs and to understand the social and eco-nomic environment in which business opportunities exist. As no less a sage than Adam Smith, the 18th century proponent of laissez faire market mechanisms, observed, there is a place for govern-ment intervention in providing basic elementary education for all, on the premise that an educated populace would make better decisions and thus assist the "invisible hand" on behalf of eco-nomic growth and public well-being.

Chapter Twelve
Humanitarian Aid

> *"In the field of world policy I would dedicate this Nation to the policy of the good neighbor — the neighbor who resolutely respects himself and, because he does so, respects the rights of neighbors.".*
>
> Franklin D. Roosevelt First Inaugural address March 4, 1933

The civilian segment of our National Service program should closely coordinate with existing aid organizations, including the Peace Corps, and possibly with the U.S. Agency for International Development/International Relief and Development (USAID/IRD), AmeriCorps VISTA, and Teach for America. Possibly participation in one of these organizations could fulfill the universal service requirement in our program, or it could be used as credit toward that obligation. Another possibility is that once our program has been established, the government would discontinue some of these others to avoid duplication and reduce administrative costs. Some of the ways in which existing humanitarian and development programs may work together are described in this chapter.

Economy of Force

Military and national security reporter Thom Shanker wrote in the January 26, 2012 *New York Times*, that today's military is primarily engaged in "economy of force" missions. This involves sending "small numbers from the American military to set up installations in far-flung regions of interest, where they can be joined by personnel from other arms of the United States government, including the State, Justice, Agriculture, and Commerce Departments; Customs and Border Protection; and the Agency for International Development."[165]

Typical of these installations is Camp Lemonnier, located in Djibouti on the Horn of Africa. Shanker notes that "the day-to-day work at Camp Lemonnier focuses on quiet efforts at improving the abilities of local militaries and law-enforcement personnel to protect and police their own territory, while assisting in building schools, digging wells, laying roads, and vaccinating livestock."[167] In this way the installation preserves an American military presence and protects national security, while providing valuable humanitarian services, all at relatively low cost. Surely our National Service corpsmen could be an economical source of manpower at installations like these all around the globe.

End of Poverty

U.S. economist Jeffrey Sachs was a previous Director of the United Nations Millennium Project, a global effort to reduce extreme poverty, hunger, and disease wherever it exists in the world. Launched at a summit meeting of some 150 national leaders, the project set forth eight Millennium Development Goals to be achieved by 2015. Sachs as leader of the effort to implement these goals considered them the number one global priority.[166]

Regrettably, our great country has not even been able to meet its financial pledge of 0.7 percent of GDP, let alone provide support personnel to effect an end to the causes of extreme poverty. In fact the whole notion of Millennial Goals is seldom if ever mentioned in political discourse in the U.S. It's difficult not to agree with Salil Shetty, Director of the United Nations Millennial Campaign, who decried the contrast, after decades of deliberations, between the huge sums spent by the U.S. and other developed nations in bailing out the banks who drove us into the Great Recession, and the inability of these same nations to make similar investments in ending or drastically reducing worldwide poverty — a goal that the campaign leaders saw as quite attainable within their timeframe.[167]

This would be a natural subject for discussion at the outset of our compulsory National Service, as well as an opportunity for boots-on-the-ground kinds of activities in which our humanitarian service personnel could be engaged. After a tour in our program, an enlightened youth would demand more from their officials, help them achieve the goals, and see them through to completion over as many economic ups and downs and election cycles as it may take.

Expanding Responsibilities for U.S. Marines

New York Times reporter, James Dao, describing changes within the U.S. Marine Corps, said that its newest recruitment campaign was focused on "something the world has in endless supply — chaos."[168] From the Corps' perspective, no matter where the next global hot spot would be, it would engage Marines. But their jobs will become broader in scope. "The new campaign will also include much information and dramatic footage of Marines delivering humanitarian aid to nations beleaguered by war, famine or natural disaster, like Haiti, where 2200 Marines provided medical supplies, food and security after the 2010 earthquake."[168]

Dao went on to explain that the emphasis on humanitarian aid is "partly the result of a national online survey conducted by JWT, the marketing firm, showing that many young adults consider 'helping people in need, wherever they may live,' an important component of good citizenship."[170] Brigadier General Joseph Osterman, Commanding General for Marine Corps Recruiting Command at the time, told Dao," 'There is a subset of Millennials who believe that the military is an avenue of service to others, not only in our nation, but also in others faced with tyranny and injustice.'"[168]

Imagine how much more humanitarian aid of this type we could provide with the huge force of participants in our program, both the military and civilian elements. Think, for example, of the help we could have provided to the Philippines in the aftermath of their horrific November 2013 typhoon experience. Or the December 2004 Indian Ocean tsunami that killed hundreds of thousands of natives and tourists and wiped away scores of towns and villages in Indonesia, Thailand, and Sumatra.

Peace Corps

In setting up the civilian service aspect of a National Service program, the sterling example of the Peace Corps naturally comes to mind, though there are some decided differences between them. Peace Corps workers come as volunteers. They are almost always college graduates with bachelor's degrees; some even have advanced degrees, facility in a second language, as well as work experience. And the great majority of them sign up because they already have a commitment to serve. By contrast, the National Service program is designed to conscript mostly 18-year-old high school graduates, with only a small minority having some higher education credits. Therefore, unlike Peace Corps volunteers, National Service participants would need additional training to be effective. Even with training, the productivity of the average National Service person would not measure up to that of the average Peace Corps volunteer.

No matter. There is a great deal of needed development aid that National Service can provide, perhaps involving more physical activity (e. g. construction, farming, care-giving) than some of the assignments taken on by Peace Corps volunteers. We should expect many similar positive outcomes both for the service corpsman and for the aid recipients. That's because the mission of our service will be similar to that of the Peace Corps, which is: "To help the people of interested countries in meeting their need for trained men and women. To help promote a better understanding of Americans on the part of the peoples served. To help promote a better understanding of other peoples on the part of Americans."

To be sure, the civilian aid and development segment of the National Service program will undoubtedly entail a large helping of boredom, physical discomfort, and perhaps resentment at times, as does our present military service. But on balance, if the Peace Corps experience is any indicator, the two years spent by National Service humanitarians will, for many of the participants, be the fastest and most satisfying time of their lives.

As Dillon Banerjee, former Peace Corps volunteer in Cameroon, West Africa, says in *The Insider's Guide to the Peace Corps*, "Know that you are about to discover new things about the world, about others, and about yourself."[169] He goes on to say that "Peace Corps training is an experience in and of itself. It is three months (give or take) of making new friends, taking new steps, learning about a different culture, and learning about yourself. It pampers you and challenges you, informs you and confuses you, allows you to grow but shelters you. Most importantly, it prepares you for two years on your own in an environment more foreign and exciting than any you've ever encountered."[170]

Those lucky enough to be taught a foreign language as part of their Peace Corps training will benefit additionally from one of the best language training programs in the world. Banerjee explains that "Rather than the conventional method of starting with vocabulary drills, verb conjugations, and personal pronoun memorization, trainees engage in direct dialog with native speakers from day one."[171] Depending on their assigned destination, the typical Peace Corps language trainee will learn French, Spanish, Portuguese, or Swahili.

Banerjee goes on to describe other aspects of Peace Corps training that provide a high level of competence. "Technical training focuses on practical skills as opposed to theory or policy. If you're an agro-forester, you'll spend the majority of your training time on a farm or demonstration plot getting your hands dirty. If you're a teacher, you'll spend lots of time in front of peers, students, and trainers honing your teaching skills. If you're a health worker, you'll practice giving presentations on health-related subjects in the local language. In many ways, once you reach your village, you'll feel as though you've already racked up substantive experience and won't be as intimidated as you initially anticipated." [172] If you are thinking that these types of training and experience are fine for college-graduated Peace Corps volunteers, but beyond the capabilities of the average 18-year-old service person, think again. On a need to know basis, our current military service provides many 18-year-olds with very similar types of training in languages, equipment maintenance, mechanics, and electronics.

The reasons for establishing this National Service program and the reasons underlying the founding of the Peace Corps are remarkably similar. Sargent Shriver, who helped President Kennedy create the Peace Corps in 1961, and went on to become its first director, once told his son Tim Shriver that when the founders started the Peace Corps, they realized they were gambling everything on an idea that had never been tried before. The younger Shriver recalls his father saying, "They were risking their professional reputations and careers, risking the credibility of the

President of the United States, risking young people's lives and the country's reputation in the middle of the Cold War, on an idea that to many seemed foolish. The idea of risk is so tied to the idea of greatness — you cannot be great without risking yourself....

"That idea of taking big risks for big gains, to do big things that would be truly sustainable, for us and for others, said Shriver, 'is gone from our public life now. Now it is all about split the difference, triangulate, and just get me 51 percent.' " [173] How pertinent this observation is today, 50 years later, when we look at the dysfunction and lack of action in Washington.

Perhaps I am an irrepressible optimist, but I predict that this will change. A leader will come along with the drive and passion to propose, champion, and implement a program of this nature. This leader will have the courage to take big risks to indeed pursue and advocate for a National Service program. There is a chance that he or she will experience not only significant opposition in the voting booth from political foes, but could in fact even be exposed to organized, sometimes violent, groups that will rise up to oppose them: Mothers Against Drafting Our Children, Citizens Against Conscription , and various other factions who will cite the Constitution as their basis of opposition, however farfetched their interpretation of what that document truly says.

This yet-to-arise national advocate for National Service will think, as Sargent Shriver did, "that if we created a program like the Peace Corps, that would offer young Americans the chance to work for nothing, live in adverse conditions, help others, and build relationships, everyone would want to do that. They actually thought everyone would want to work for nothing to help poor people and, in the process, help themselves....that Americans all didn't just want to file their taxes — that people wanted to give to their country, they didn't just want to get from it. They want to be part of something larger — to believe in ideas that can change the course of their lives and even history itself."[173] Reader...how about you?

This all makes a lot of sense to me. Most people I know do indeed want to give to their country. Sometimes this desire shows on the surface, as in the case of our many honest and dedicated public servants whom we often overlook when blinded by the glare of our many selfish greedy and corrupt officials. Sometimes the desire is hidden just waiting to spring forth with encouragement offered by opportunities such as the Peace Corps. It's not just Dillon Banerjee who found his Peace Corps training life-changing and life-affirming. So have hundreds of others who tell their positive stories in the *Peace Corps Passport*, the Corps' newsletter.

With this in mind I decided to get some first-hand accounts from friends and acquaintances who had served.

One of them is **David Hopkins**, a 1962 Yale graduate who served in Turkey after graduation, and then went on to a very successful business career as a program manager for IBM. Here in paraphrased form is our brief interview.

- What prompted you to join the Peace Corps, and did you also consider the military?

  Peace Corps was very much in the limelight then and I was tired of studying, and wanted a new experience, but not a military one.

- What was your assignment(s) and how much choice did you have?

  I was assigned to teach English in a Turkish town. Had I not accepted that offer, I would have been given one or two more choices, and if I declined those, they would have assumed I was not Peace Corps material.

- What did you take away from your exposure to a different culture and how did that help in your personal development?

I received training in Turkish history, Islamic beliefs and culture, and a certain amount of physical training to prepare me for my assignment. But there is nothing like spending two years living amongst a people, on the local economy, in a foreign language and a foreign culture, with only one or two other Americans around, to gain not only a good understanding of the other culture, but also a better understanding of one's own place in the world, and how better to deal with the world in the future.

I think this is a fairly typical reaction of those who served their two-year term and got out. Of course there were also many who elected to continue on in foreign service.

- What changes in your perception of our American values or culture resulted from the Peace Corps experience?

I saw plenty of evidence that American and Western customs have impacted Turkish culture, and that individual Turks were interested in what goes on here, but there has been very little cultural impact in reverse until the past ten years or so. Now there are many evidences of Turkish culture in this country

Dave noted that unfortunately the Peace Corps involvement in Turkey was rather short-lived because of differences in the expectations of the Turkish authorities and those of the Peace Corps.

Most of the Peace Corps volunteers in David Hopkins' day were college graduates, so he found it difficult to compare his experience with the kinds of service our 18-year-old corpsmen might provide. But he directed me to a report in the *News Times* of Danbury, CT published in February 2011 in which many other positive experiences of Peace Corps volunteers were recounted. One young lady, a graduate of UC Berkeley with a degree in American history and politics, taught English in a small Turkish town on the Black Sea. She described her tour as a very positive learning experience in spite of the challenges of adjusting to and working in a society lacking some basic women's rights. Another Peace Corps volunteer with a master's degree in public health was assigned a public health education role in Paraguay. He was diverted somewhat from his original assignment when he became involved in spearheading the establishment of a successful new women-owned bakery, but all in all I would see his experience also as a positive one.

David Hopkins, as one might expect and would surely hope, continues his volunteer activities throughout his retirement years. He and his wife Janet edited and published our local Sherman, CT newspaper for many years, he has served on and chaired various town commissions, and run for First Selectman. David is truly a "pillar of the community".

Barbara and Denis Curtiss, whom I also interviewed, described their experience in the Peace Corps by echoing its motto "the toughest job you'll ever love." They joined the Peace Corps in 1976 at the age of 30 for the standard two-year stint. Prior to that Barbara had been a social worker, Denis a sculptor and antiques restorer. Barbara, having traveled considerably in her earlier years, was looking for a change with adventure overseas, as was Denis. And change they got! The couple was assigned to the Pacific island country of Fiji where, after brief indoctrination and training in the language and customs of the

Fijians, they took up residence among the natives and started their assignments, Barbara teaching English and Denis industrial arts. Their community development efforts were challenging to say the least. Students were willing and pleasant, but not prepared to absorb the lessons Barbara and Denis were assigned to teach. Medicine practiced by witch doctors, and scary primitive rituals, the sort most of us see only in *National Geographic*, were commonplace. Efforts to circumvent the system were only marginally successful and rather frustrating.

Some customs within their new community taught Barbara and Denis humbling lessons. For examples, their hosts treated outsiders as welcome guests, not as intruders as we so often do. Fijians were also fastidious in their dress and cleanliness, all the more visible when compared with the slovenly appearance of some of the Peace Corps volunteers.

Barbara and Denis immersed themselves in their new community, learned to love their hosts, and were appreciated, respected, and loved in return. When their Peace Corps assignment ended, they left with a sense that they had received much more than they had given. Of course they also had a new appreciation for their homeland and the opportunities afforded Americans when compared with the rest of the world.

Like all returning Peace Corps volunteers, the Curtiss' were given a leg up when interviewing for employment back home. Typically, a note about their service on their resume moved them to the front of the applicants' line. Employers appreciated the fact that they were able to deal with unusual challenges. If there was a negative to Peace Corps service, it was the tremendous letdown that many of their colleagues experienced when returning home to "their world" after such an emotionally and intellectually stimulating period of exploration and discovery abroad.

When **Sharon Demado** graduated from Mary Washington College in Virginia with a business degree, she wasn't at all sure what her next step should be. Something different, challenging, and involving travel appealed to her, and she decided to enter the Peace Corps in 2005. While she hoped to be assigned to a Spanish-speaking country in South or Central America and to become fluent in the language, the Peace Corps had other ideas. They assigned her to Gambia, a tiny nation on the west coast of Africa, where extensive logging and desertification were rapidly degrading the environment. As part of her preparation stateside, Sharon and her colleagues were trained in tree planting for reforestation and in irrigation and other farming practices, including beekeeping, all of which they were to demonstrate once they arrived in their new communities. She was also taught the native language, Pular.

Sharon was assigned by herself to a small village of 70-80 persons and moved into her host family's primitive quarters, which had neither running water nor electricity. In spite of the difficult conditions, she found her assignment very rewarding, and once fluent in Pular, had a degree of success teaching tree-planting and beekeeping skills. However, she does think that, had there been at least one more Peace Corps volunteer assigned with her to that village, much more could have been accomplished.

All in all it was a very positive two-way experience learning their culture and teaching ours. Would she do it all over again? Sharon told me that not only would she, but she will…when she retires. At present she lives in Naugatuck, CT and is an emergency room nurse at Charlotte Hungerford Hospital in Torrington.

Scott Yurcheshen now works with the federal government in Washington. Like many others, he was uncertain of a career path after college and, rather than continuing in an aimless job, joined the Peace Corps to do something more worthwhile as he figured out his future. His experience had some positive outcomes, but with a downside, as well.

His assignment was in business development on the outer island of Ovaka, part of the archipelago of the Kingdom of Tonga in the South Pacific. While that location was not one of Scott's choices, the Peace Corps did make an effort to accommodate his wishes regarding the specific task. When asked about his takeaways, he said that the change from his home environment to "living in a poor country without the amenities of America allowed me to better understand and empathize with others."

Scott learned that any progress he made in Ovaka depended on, as he had frequently been told by colleagues, developing and cultivating relationships with the people in his community. This was a very positive experience from the standpoint of learning to adapt to challenging and uncomfortable situations. Though he sometimes questioned his original decision to join the Peace Corps, he learned perseverance in managing difficult stressful times. Still, Scott regards his work as less fruitful than he had hoped for. Unlike volunteers with whom he and I have spoken who were assigned to other countries, Scott did not find much to respect or appreciate in the Tongan culture itself.

After his tour, Scott went on to graduate school in Australia as a Peace Corps fellow, where he worked with many other international students expanding his view of the world and other cultures. The experience of being abroad was extremely valuable. However, while he generally agrees with the concept of the Peace Corps, he told me that its funding, support system, and program organization all need significant improvement, and without those he does not consider it a wholly satisfactory model for our National Service program.

AmeriCorps VISTA

Volunteers in Service to America or VISTA is an anti-poverty and job-training program that came out of Lyndon Johnson's Economic Opportunity Act of 1964. Created as the domestic version of Kennedy's Peace Corps, VISTA recruits volunteers who are willing to dedicate a year's service, working for a host non-profit organization or a municipal agency or organization such as a school, a church, a community center, a head start program, or a clinic. In return for their service, VISTA volunteers are provided orientation, travel expenses, and living allowances sufficient to keep them at the same poverty level as the people they serve, the better to relate to the people they live with and serve. VISTA workers also receive separation money to be used toward college tuition when their year is over. During the Clinton administration, VISTA was brought under the newly-created AmeriCorps program, a division of the Corporation for National and Community Service, and was renamed AmeriCorps VISTA.

AmeriCorps VISTA, while previously enjoying strong bi-partisan support, is now under the same sort of budget-cutting pressure as many other federal and state social service and anti-poverty programs. The intent was to have 140,000 members serving projects like building low income housing, cleaning up rivers and parks, responding to natural disasters with FEMA and teaching at-risk students. However, the actual number of domestic AmeriCorps VISTA volunteers has come down from its high of 88,000 in 2010, with a strong likelihood that it will continue to shrink further in the near future. This is indeed unfortunate considering the fine work done by its volunteers, and the positive impact on both the volunteers and the communities served.

The experience of **Nicholas Murphy** with whom I communicated was quite similar to those of the Peace Corps volunteers mentioned previously. Nicholas is of Mexican descent, adopted at birth by his American parents, and right after college graduation in 1999, with no career path in mind, joined AmeriCorps. In his own words, he had "grown up in a rather sheltered small town in Connecticut….I was painfully aware of looking and being 'different'. AmeriCorps offered me a chance to get off on my own and live independently…while I figured things out." He chose to work in Albuquerque, New Mexico which has a large Mexican-American population, and he was assigned to work at a new Community Center in a high crime part of the city. He set up and ran an after school program for young Mexican-Americans that also involved reaching out to their parents, many of whom did not speak English. The program was underfunded , so Nicholas had to "scavenge for supplies, books and equipment", and he said "I discovered strengths I never knew I had and I learned that some of my childhood feelings of insecurity could be channeled into making me a natural mentor and athletic coach for these kids." When given some added responsibilities, he signed on for a second year, and when he left the program, he knew he was "destined to work with children, teaching, coaching, and mentoring troubled boys." Nicholas attributes the confidence and maturity gained from his AmeriCorps years to making him a better citizen, and he is proud to have given something back to his country. He now splits his time between mentoring troubled boys for the department of Youth Services in the New Haven, Connecticut area, coaching soccer and basketball for the West Haven Parks and Recreation Department, and running his landscaping business in Kent Connecticut.

AmeriCorps naysayers point to anecdotal shortcomings. James Bovard, in a *Wall Street Journal* opinion piece, cited AmeriCorps recruits releasing balloons to draw attention to the plight of abused children; a hip-hop poetry competition at the Institute for Study and Practice of Nonviolence in Providence, Rhode Island; a trivia night at a Texas bar to promote public service; puppet shows supporting recycling, and so on.

Regardless, even these rather innocent, possibly ill-conceived, events would certainly seem to have redeeming benefits in the promotion of public service and awareness. I am far more inclined to go with the supportive opinions of Presidents Bill Clinton and Barack Obama. Clinton declared that AmeriCorps "is 'living proof' that if we all hold hands and believe we're going into the future together, we can change anything we want to change."[174] And President Obama said that AmeriCorps "embodies the best of our nation's history, diversity, and commitment to service."[174] Even Bovard allowed that, in spite of a lack of appropriate supervision and funding, they should be given credit for the constructive achievements of their volunteers — for example building levees in the flooded Midwest and aiding victims of Oklahoma tornadoes.[174] Many will make the argument that we should not expect a government-mandated universal National Service program to be better- or even equally well- supervised and managed than the government-supported AmeriCorps service organization. I would contend otherwise. Our program, by the very nature of its mandatory and universal aspect, will be much more transparent and accountable to the taxpayer. Sure, there will be problems with inefficiencies and waste, as there are now with our volunteer military services. But, just as we now can boast that our military is the finest in the world, so we will be able to boast that we also have the finest universal service organization.

U.S. Agency for International Development (USAID)

We constantly complain, and understandably so, that a good deal of the financial aid we provide other countries for political or humanitarian purposes does not reach the intended recipients, but is siphoned off as graft to local administrators. Inefficiencies and waste also eat up too large a portion of foreign aid and development funds.

Dion Nissenbaum, writing for *The Wall Street Journal*, addressed the origins of USAID established by President John F. Kennedy in 1961. The agency functioned as a key financial aid to developing nations, and, after the September 11, 2001 terrorist attack, the Bush administration changed its mission to compliment our middle east military objectives and to support our large rebuilding project in Iraq.[175] The results have been disappointing, to say the least.

Not surprisingly the same thing is happening in the $85 billion reconstruction program in Afghanistan, and for many of the same reasons, including an insurgency, cost overruns primarily due to massive security, and corruption.[175]

USAID funds for road construction were funneled through non-governmental organization IRD (International Relief and Development), whose stated mission is to "reduce the suffering of the world's most vulnerable groups and provide the tools and resources needed to improve their self-sufficiency." Theirs is a noble mission indeed, but like the plans of so many well-intended NGOs it is subject to inefficiencies and abuse inherent in operating within developing nations.

Case in point is the $400 million paid by the U.S., China, and NATO to an Afghan entrepreneur, Ajmal Hasas, to build 1,200 miles of road in the remote province of Badghis in northwestern Afghanistan. The road would connect landlocked western China and several Central Asian countries with Iranian seaports and world markets. The only problem was that with most of the money spent, only 100 miles were completed, and USAID officials had no choice but to shut down the vast "Road to Nowhere," leaving provincial authorities and investors angry and disappointed.

What's the alternative? Should we stop doling out money when there is limited control over how it is used? I would contend that we cannot abandon this tool. For all its vulnerabilities, investments of this kind are essential if we wish to curry favor with developing nations and lead them to a path of peace, non-aggression, and, in some cases, democracy. We must show them by example that we are indeed friendly and supportive. To do this we should send our most valuable resource, our National Service program youth, to work with them on specific projects with specific missions and specific timetables. At the same time we must improve our record on financial oversight of the projects in which we invest.

If we do this we are more likely to get the kind of reaction from the locals that says, *Hey, these guys are just like us. They are friendly and helpful. Uncle Sam does indeed have our best interests at heart.* Isn't this a more valuable tool to promote our ideals than the disappointment and anger that follows a failed or substandard project? USAID is apparently coming around to this notion themselves according to Nissenbaum who says that, as a result of the ill-conceived "Road to Nowhere," USAID is shifting its attention to smaller more manageable programs and away from the large projects that have been so difficult to control.

These new programs tend to be smaller in scope and are heavily weighted toward agricultural development, the income source for 75 percent of Afghans. They are aimed at training farmers in improved production practices, particularly the growing of high-value crops and livestock; at increasing post-harvest technologies and storage capacities for greater food security and off- season sales; at showing women ways to market home-grown foods and to adopt better nutrition for their families; lastly, USAID assists the Afghan government in formulating modern and enforceable agricultural policies. The hope, of course, is that they will eventually be able to manage on their own.[177] Surely this type of project could efficiently use the assistance of our National Service program youth at a fraction of the cost of subcontracted private profit-oriented companies.

Teach for America

The idea of putting federal funding into attracting high-quality college graduates to teach for a few years before entering their chosen career paths was first proposed by President Lyndon Johnson in 1964. The Teacher Corps, as it was called, was a key element of his Great Society, a collection of domestic social reform programs. The goal of the Teacher Corps was to remedy the teacher shortage in poorer school districts, particularly in inner cities and in rural districts, and through that means to work toward eliminating poverty, inequality and racial injustice in the U.S. The Teacher Corps became a reality the following year when Congress passed funding legislation. Despite considerable success, the Corps was replaced in 1981 by a program of block grants to needy schools.

The basic concept of the Teacher Corps was revived in 1990 when Wendy Kopp, herself a recent college graduate, founded Teach for America as a non-profit privately-funded organization. She recruited an initial class of 500 high-achieving college graduates committed to teaching for two years in low-income communities in the U.S. According to the organization's figures for the 2015-2016 school year, it has 19,000 corps members currently teaching in 53 regions of the country. Of these teachers, half identify as people of color . Additionally, 48 percent are from low-income backgrounds with one in three being the first in their family to graduate from college. One in five have backgrounds in science, technology, engineering or math, the teaching areas often hardest to fill. Another 32,000 alumni continue to be part of the wider Teach for American community, with impacts as educational leaders and advocates. Teach for America has also spawned Teach for All, a global network of over 35 independent, locally led and funded partner organizations serving in disadvantaged impoverished communities throughout the world.[176]

The National Service program I envision could team up with

these organizations to place talented 18-year-old corpsmen in needy schools as assistants to professional teachers. Alternatively, the students would be allowed to defer their service commitment in order to complete their college work, but they would have to sign a contract when they enter college, committing them to teach for at least two years after graduation. This would be similar to the commitment incoming freshmen make for post-college service when they enter one of the military academies, albeit National Service would require a somewhat shorter total commitment.

Global Health Corps

Barbara Bush, daughter of President George W. Bush, was overwhelmed by the effects of AIDS on the Ugandans when she visited their country with her father who was so responsible for taking the steps to the eventual decline of AIDS worldwide. She took this all to heart, continued her studies at Yale focusing on health, and then took a job in a South African hospital where she worked with children suffering from AIDS. With this background, she started Global Health Corps as an organization to provide worldwide education in health issues. While Global Health Corps in 2015 offered less than 150 fellowships, it receives almost 6000 applications yearly.[177]

Religious Affiliated Service

In addition to charitable and/or government-sponsored relief and development organizations, many young people now participate in similarly dedicated programs sponsored by their religious affiliations. Consideration should be given to allowing such service to qualify as participation in the civilian aspect of our National Service program. This would, of course, run into the issue of separation of church and state, and I'm not sure it could be satisfactorily resolved, but it's worth examining further. Even in Israel, the national compulsory service wrestles with allowing participation in their advanced religious studies to qualify. (More on this will follow in Chapter Fifteen.)

The missionaries of the Mormon faith demonstrate that the desire to serve is strong in many of us. While not all of our 18-year-olds will look forward to participating in our National Service program, I think we will find a strong desire to serve here also. The Mormon Church's program is entirely dependent on volunteers, currently numbering approximately 52,000 "serving in 405 missions around the world. They proselytize in every country where the government and political climate allow it."[178] Mormon missionaries are passionate about serving their faith or simply serving mankind, and our National Service corpsmen, if properly indoctrinated, should also have or find an equal passion in serving their country or mankind.

The Mormon Church recently increased the participation of their young men by lowering the eligible age from 19 years to 18 years, thus facilitating those youngsters who wish to enter right after high school and before college. Similarly the church has lowered the age for women participants from 21 to 19, because by age 21 many Mormon women are married, working, or pursuing further education. As a result, many more women now volunteer.[179] Education continues throughout the Mormon mission years, starting with a few weeks of training and language immersion before setting out on their assignment, somewhat similar to what takes place in our National Service program.

You might say this has no bearing on our National Service program because these Mormon youngsters are volunteers, whereas our participants will be conscripts. The Mormons are raised to have a certain passion for their work, but ultimately they must go where they are needed and that is often somewhere other than their preference. While they are missionaries, they work full time with one-half day off weekly to take care of cleaning, writing letters, and recreation. They are permitted to call home only a couple of times per year and must communicate with loved ones only by mail and e-mail the rest of the year. [180] Does this sound familiar to any of you who have served in the military?

According to LDS spokespersons, many missionaries grow to love the areas in which they serve so much that they find it harder to come home after the missions are over than it was for them to leave in the first place. They return home as informed ambassadors of the nations and cultures where they served.[178] Those serving in the civilian and international service parts of our National Service program will undoubtedly have similar reactions. Our program should produce whole generations of international ambassadors building an appreciation for other nations and cultures, while at the same time spreading a gospel of freedom.

Military Involvement

Our existing military already spreads this gospel of freedom and a great deal of good will throughout the Middle East and other parts of the world and this goes a long way to counter the perception of those who see us only as invaders and occupiers.

A perfect example of this is represented by Lieutenant Colonel William R. McKern, who sent a message to my community church about his positive relationship with his Muslim host during deployment in Iraq. Through friendship he developed with Abu Sajjad , the man in charge of the local mosque, McKern organized a group of soldiers to help with a variety of much needed improvements to the mosque. Impressed with this positive experience, Colonel McKern thought an interfaith dialog would be beneficial to the Americans and Iraqis in the area. With Abu Sajjad's assistance, he was able to arrange a very productive meeting and tour of the mosque with the local Muslim imam and the Christian and Jewish chaplains. A lengthy discussion of religion, politics, history, and culture by the participants ensued, and Colonel McKern looks back on this day as quite understandably the best that he'd experienced during his tour in Iraq. I'm sure there are many similar relations being built on a daily basis that help to counteract the misconceptions of America's motives in other parts of the world, and I can only imagine the additional good that would result from the presence of our National Service program good-will ambassadors, military and civilian, throughout the globe.

Reflections on a Rite of Passage

Thinking about all these humanitarian aid organizations that work to bring assistance and improvements to developing countries leads me to reflect on the rite of passage that most high school seniors are faced with: college admissions. One option that all too few college applicants consider is the opportunity afforded by some colleges and universities to spend a Gap Year between high school graduation and their freshman year. The Gap Year is typically spent studying abroad, immersed in and getting acquainted with unfamiliar culture. If you speak with college students and graduates who have partaken of this opportunity, you will find an almost unanimous favorable reaction to the experience. In many cases these Gap Year students have learned a foreign language or improved their ability in a language already studied. They have witnessed art that perhaps they cannot see in American museums, and gazed upon architectural creations quite different from anything they are used to in their rural, suburban, or urban settings at home. They eat and drink new and different foods and beverages, become aware of different daily routines and religious practices, and, if boarding with a family in a private home abroad, have the opportunity to participate in unfamiliar customs and routines. They become acquainted with economies, government, and politics that in many cases are quite different from capitalism and democracy at home. And they may be rather amazed that their hosts know more about our government and elected officials than we do about theirs, or in many cases than we do about our own!

More significant than the details of the international experience is the lifelong benefit of developing a much more open-minded and tolerant attitude toward people, cultures, and governments with which we traditionally disagree, perhaps dislike, or at a minimum tend to patronize.

Now, think about those college graduates who did not spend a year abroad. Ask them what they think about a semester or year abroad. More often than not, you will find that they wish they had had that experience.

All of these advantages and benefits would apply to some degree to many of our National Service program participants, though probably not to the same degree that they would to a college student. Some in the military National Service stationed overseas would have a certain amount of liberty and leave time to experience their surroundings. For example, if some of those serving with the Sixth Fleet in the Mediterranean were participating in our program's two-year service term, they would have time to at least be introduced to some of the great cities on or near the Mediterranean coast. Then too, many of those in the civilian element overseas would probably have greater exposure to their new surroundings and an experience more comparable to that of college students studying abroad or during a Gap Year.

Chapter Thirteen
Desire for Change

> *Never doubt that a small group of thoughtful com-*
> *mitted citizens can change the world; indeed, it's the*
> *only thing that ever has.*
>
> Margaret Mead - American cultural anthropologist

Just as the military fosters camaraderie among those who serve, I think we can expect National Service to foster its own kind of camaraderie. The sheer number of participants who would be involved gives them a unique opportunity to address and correct social, economic and environmental ills, not only through the ballot box, but also in all those in-between times when issues of public concern arise and petitioning government is a means of forcing change. Perhaps they would join their own kind of veterans' organization, enjoying lifelong associations with people who had shared their experiences.

Look at the changes that concerned groups have made simply by working through Change.org, a free social activism and petitioning tool launched in California in 2007. Its stated mission is to alter the balance of power between individuals and large organizations and to transform their communities, locally, nationally, and globally through concerted action. Today there are more than

100 million Change.org users in 196 countries, mobilizing like-minded citizens to speak out on issues of injustice, corruption, prison reform, animal rights, child pornography, environmental degradation, and usurpations of individual rights. One petition on Change.org gathered 86,000 signatures calling for Backpage.com to stop accepting adult ads that had been cited in promoting sex traffic. A 306,000 signature petition on Change.org was instrumental in convincing Bank of America to rescind a new $5-a-month fee for the use of their debit cards. A similar 160,000 signature petition was instrumental in persuading Verizon to back down from its $2 charge for paying certain bills online. This is living proof that any group, once they develop the habit of working cooperatively, can initiate and expedite changes that our elected officials have either failed to address on their own or are prohibited from taking on directly.[181] And they can do it — "going viral" on some really hot issues, almost as fast as the blink of an eye.

There is untold untapped power in this mobilization. Steve Phillips made the case in his New York Times article "How to Build a Democratic Majority", published in October 2016 shortly before the elections. Phillips argued that money spent on mobilization, i.e. direct mail, door to door canvassing, social media and other personal contact, is far more effective than money spent on advertising in political action or election campaigns. And, as it turned out, he was proven correct, apparently to his dismay, as he was attempting to persuade the Democrats to follow his recommendations. Hillary Clinton vastly outspent Donald Trump on campaign advertising, whereas Mr. Trump's populist agenda was transmitted at relatively little cost via more direct routes, in particular his incessant "tweets", to the individuals whose cause aligned more closely with his. [182]

Ralph Nader in his book *Breaking Through Power* also addresses how to effect change. An outsider by nature, Nader dismisses Political Action Committees or PACs with huge advertising budgets as agents of change. He favors small committed groups from no more than one percent of the active citizenry backed up by majority public opinion to break through the power of big government, big corporate influence and big money, and to effect major change. The focus of his agenda for these small civic groups, as one might assume, includes gaining airtime on the public airwaves, defending and extending civil liberties, enforcing the Constitution on war-making decisions, giving taxpayers "standing" to sue the government in court, and, in general, confronting Wall Street and corporate crime. Nader claims that all that is required to take action and accomplish goals in each of the 435 Congressional Districts is to apply at least 200 hours of volunteer work in each of the districts to setup and support an office with at least four full-time workers. The initial goals would be to establish direct working relationships with their Representative and Senators and to mobilize the public to promote their agenda.[183]

Time for the Millennials

Tom Friedman, writing about the 2013 government shutdown said, "Short of an economic meltdown, there is only one thing that might produce meaningful change: a mass movement for tax, spending and entitlement reform led by the cohort that is the least organized but will be the most affected if we don't think long term — today's young people."[184] Friedman refers to a college speaking tour by Stan Druckenmiller, the legendary investor who predicted the subprime bust. Mr. Druckenmiller cited his generation's bringing down the president in the '60s because they didn't want to go into the war against Vietnam as an example of the power of young people.

Tom Friedman notes that government spending, investments, and entitlements have overwhelmingly benefited the elderly since the 1960s and it will only get more lopsided, leading to a huge tax burden on the young. Without greater economic growth, these policies will necessitate cutting the very government invest-ments in infrastructure, Head Start, and medical and technology research that help the poorest and also create jobs of the future. Friedman shares with Druckenmiller and his speaking partner Geoffrey Canada, the conviction "that only a Vietnam-war-scale movement by the young can break through the web of special in-terests to force politicians to put in place the reforms that would actually secure both today's seniors and future seniors, today's middle class and the wanna-be middle class."[184]

And, it is apparent that the younger generation, the so-called Millennials born in 1981 or thereafter, are indeed a generation for change. As Charle Blow pointed out in his *New York Times* article "The Young Are Restless," their "views on a broad range of policy issues are so different from older Americans' perspectives that they are likely to reshape the political dialogue faster than the political class can catch up."[187] Drawing from a Pew Research Center Poll on social and demographic trends, Blow found that a majority of Millennials support same-sex marriage. According to a separate Gallup report, members of the Millennial genera-tion are least likely to own guns. They are also the least religious, with more than a quarter of them specifying no religious affilia-tion at all, and they are the most racially diverse group. According to Mr. Blow's resources, only "Fifty-eight percent of voters under 30 were white non-Hispanic in 2012, down from 74 percent in 2000 ….[and these] younger Americans are thirsty for change that lines up with their more liberal cultural worldview."[185]

Now one might say, well, if they're so liberal, might they not pro-test universal conscription? Yes, they probably would in large numbers, were the program to offer only the military option, but my educated guess is that that they will rally around this change because it fundamentally alters the traditional imbalance between the few dictating to the many and fosters a new climate where all truly participate in their nation's destiny.

The Next Influentials

While only an early part of the National Service program curriculum is educational in the traditional book learning sense, there is an enormous educational element provided by two years of association with other young men and women of a similar age from all walks of life. Add to this the trade school type of educational opportunities available from the military service option; the exposure to other cultures offered by the international humanitarian aid option;, and the environmental stewardship offered by the program's civilian service option, and we will indeed provide our youth with an invaluable educational and development experience. I see this educated youth as our next major voting bloc, soon to become more influential than Wall Street, the pharmaceutical lobby, the American Medical Association, AARP, the Association of Trial Lawyers, the Right to Life group, and even the National Rifle Association.

New York Times columnist Bob Herbert, expressing a priority for a better- educated youth, has perhaps said it best: "The U.S. has not just misplaced its priorities. When the most powerful country ever to inhabit the earth finds it so easy to plunge into the horror of warfare but almost impossible to find adequate work for its people or to properly educate its young, it has lost its way entirely."[186]

Consumerism Gone Awry

The older generations and their institutions continue to hold sacred the goals of continued growth in productivity, profits, the stock market, consumption, and gross domestic product, assuming that improvements in social and environmental needs will automatically result. But we delude ourselves. Speth in *America the Possible* quotes Karl Polanyi, the Hungarian economist, from his 1944 *The Great Transformation:* "'To allow the market mechanism to be the sole director of the fate of human beings and their natural environment...would result in the demolition of society....Nature would be reduced to its elements, neighborhoods and landscapes defiled, rivers polluted, military safety jeopardized, the power to produce food and raw materials destroyed."[187]

Speth traces American consumerism to our leadership after World War II when the emphasis was on restarting the economy after years of enforced frugality and material shortages. He proposes something better-suited to America's current goals "of reducing its ecological footprint... bolstering retirement security, reducing corporate power... expanding civic engagement, focusing resources on vast social and economic disparities at home and abroad, and improving the social and psychological well-being of individuals and families."[188]

Speth calls on all of us to break the chains of consumerism and to get over a "bad case of national affluenza."[188] Consumerism, he says, now drives our growth, being approximately 70% of GDP. Consumers therefore serve our economy instead of the economy serving our consumers. This gives rise to a host of social disconnects....of getting and spending, with the longest hours on the job in the Organization for Economic Co-operation and Development (OECD), and with both parents often at work, we are neglecting the things that would truly make us better off, including personal relationships and social contact.

New Metrics for a New Kind of Prosperity

From a functional standpoint, we could start the journey away from consumerism by adding to economic prosperity (typically measured in terms of gross national product or GNP) as an index of our nation's viability another index that measures social wellness, environmental health, economic disparity, and individual happiness. As Presidential candidate Robert Kennedy said in his March 18, 1968 address at the University of Kansas, gross national product "measures everything, in short, except that which makes life worthwhile.... And it can tell us everything about Americans except why we are proud that we are Americans." For example, we would show up better with an alternate index, if we were willing to sacrifice some of the economic prosperity from expanded trade, for the protection of some of the jobs lost as a result of free trade pacts. I offer this only as one consideration when negotiating free trade pacts, not as the sole determinant as the Trump administration apparently conceives.

One possibility is the Index of Sustainable Economic Welfare (ISEW), developed in 1989 by American economist Herman Daly and theologian John Cobb, Jr.; it begins with private consumption expenditures but adjusts for non-market contributions to social welfare such as unpaid housework, and subtracts defensive expenditures such as police protection and pollution control. It also subtracts the depletion of natural resources and environmental assets.[189]

Another is the global Social Progress Index conceived in 2010 and first implemented in 2014 in order to measure social progress in areas of basic human needs, health and well-being, and personal freedom and opportunity. Currently 133 countries are assessed.

Similar measures of social progress are reported by 156 countries in the World Happiness Report initiated by a United Nations resolution in 2011 encouraging participation.

We are already seeing a movement toward more social measures of prosperity in the advent of Certified B Corporations. These are for-profit businesses which are certified by the non-profit entity B Lab on the basis of meeting rigorous and verifiable benchmarks in social and environmental performance, and commitment to sustainability in the way they operate. The idea was born among a group of American entrepreneurs and investors gathered in

Berkeley, CA in 2006, and it clearly touched a need. As of 2014 there are over 1000 certified B Corporations across 60 industries in 30 countries. The B Lab has also been a force behind the passage of supportive legislation in 26 states, plus the District of Columbia[190]

Taking on the Gun Lobby

As anticipated in Chapter Eight, the new generation participating in our National Service program will surely provide the spirit and manpower to keep gun control alive and growing for years to come.

I sincerely doubt that these voters, enlightened by their experience in National Service, would sit back and let their elected officials or candidates for office maintain near silence on the issue of gun control as so many do in the face of NRA opposition. The duplicity of the National Rifle Association's claim as "America's longest-standing civil rights organization [and as the] proud defenders of history's patriots and diligent protectors of the Second Amendment" would quickly be exposed.

While the Second Amendment allows an individual to bear arms for any purpose whatsoever, surely it cannot be disputed that one should be required to show a degree of competence, verified by background checks and training, and obtain a license for any weapons as we do to lawfully drive a car or to hunt and fish. The FDA prevents us from buying certain chemicals that are harmful to humans, and it regulates the use of many potent drugs in order to protect the public. On what basis can the NRA or anyone really say that background checks to weed out criminals and psychologically disturbed individuals inhibit their freedom?

There are rather compelling arguments from some quarters that banning assault rifles per se would not significantly reduce the threat of rampage killings. This is addressed comprehensively in *The Gun Debate* that I referenced in Chapter Eight. However, gun control being such an important issue, why hasn't the government conducted, and completed by now, a study of the causes and prevention of gun violence that addresses background checks, mental health evaluations, safety training, and weapon and magazine restrictions, and other mitigation steps, and that tests each one of these against the circumstances of each rampage shooting, say over the past 10 or 20 years. It shouldn't be too hard to determine which of the actions might have prevented or mitigated each of the rampages, and that should give us a pretty good idea of the actions most likely to have a positive effect in the future.

A similar study program should be conducted relative to gun deaths in general from homicides, suicides and accidents. We simply must insist on meaningful regulations and stand up to the resistance of the NRA.

I would see the military boot camp phase in both the military and civilian service components of our program as an opportunity for training in the proper safe use of weapons that would be very beneficial to those who choose to possess pistols or long guns when they return from their National Service.

Perhaps there will be some returning from the military component of our National Service program who would deem it perfectly appropriate when they return to private life to have uncontrolled access to all manner of personal weapons. But I conjecture that the vast majority of young people coming out of our program would surely find this totally inappropriate and would pressure their elected officials to legislate against it. At the very minimum, they would be educated enough in the dangers of these deadly weapons to demand meaningful regulations. Some of them will have seen firsthand the destructive nature of them. While a ban on any particular type of weapon per se may not reduce crime

significantly, regulations controlling the distribution of ammunition — say, in large volume only to shooting clubs, tightening
the background check procedures, and making available the safety features discussed in Chapter Eight would surely reduce the
threat.

Grass Roots, Big Money and Needed Reforms

Perhaps the most important role the voting bloc composed of
National Service graduates could play would be in taking on the
excesses of Big Money influence. One particularly important are-
na would be meaningful campaign finance reform. The Supreme
Court continues under its majority of conservative judges to tolerate unlimited campaign financing by individuals and corporations, in the name of free speech, and we are left wondering where
it will all end.

Two cases lie at the heart of the matter. The Citizens United Case,
decided in 2010, did away with overall limits on the amount corporations, associations, and unions can donate to a campaign.
Ruling that political spending is a form of protected speech under the First Amendment, and that corporations and unions are
"people," it found that they, too, were entitled to all the rights of
free speech, including the use of advertising campaigns to persuade the voting public. In McCutcheon vs. the Federal Elections
Commission, decided in 2014, the Supreme Court ruled that
while the limit donors can give to any individual candidate remains at $2,700 per fiscal year, they can give this amount to as
many candidates as they wish, again citing First Amendment
rights. If donations continue to be considered a freedom of
speech right, then surely all barriers, including the $2,700 indi-
vidual candidate limit, will eventually fall. Big Money that now
all but controls most of our national elections, the Trump presidential election being an exception, will only get bigger and
more controlling. Increasingly, the wealthy are calling the shots

while the majority of our citizens are thus effectively becoming disenfranchised.

I anticipate that as our young people benefit from the education and wider horizons gained through compulsory national service, they will build the self-esteem and political awareness needed to question the growing social and economic disparities in their country.

Surely it's a matter of interpretation. The First Amendment doesn't say "Congress shall make no law… abridging the freedom to donate unlimited funds to candidates running for political office." However, certain members of the High Court, as strict constructionists, believe that it is implied. Many of us strongly doubt that the Founding Fathers meant to protect this modern "freedom" when they wrote the First Amendment. With a ground swell movement led by our new National Service voting bloc, we can surely find and elect officials who will influence the Supreme Court to reinterpret the First Amendment. Another route would be to pass a new Constitutional amendment to put stricter limits on how politicians and lobbyists can spend their money to manipulate public opinion. That could happen if there is enough grass roots pressure to force Congress to start the process.

I also contend that this enlightened voting bloc would be in a stronger position to demand implementation of other major social and economic programs that are supported in theory by both parties, but stalled in practice by political fears of losing powerful constituencies. Prime examples of urgent national issues that need our attention are energy independence through renewable resources, reduction of greenhouse gases, conservation of our precious water resources, improved mass transit including appropriate high-speed rail service between major cities, upgrades to our system of electrical power distribution in the face of cyber and terrorist security threats, increasingly severe weather conditions resulting from climate change, and finally some long-overdue repairs and improvements to our highways, roads, bridges, and the whole complex of water transport, water storage, water treatment, and flood control facilities.

Learning to Share Globally

On a grander scale, we would hope that the exposure to and tolerance for others that participants in National Service will develop during their tour of duty will lead us not only toward greater empathy for those at home, but equally important to concerns for all humanity and for protecting and sustaining the planet. When exposed to others around the world, we will all be better able to understand that we Americans, while givers to the world of foreign aid in many forms, are also the biggest takers from the world of most of the resources that sustain life, i.e., forests, minerals, water, and non-renewable oil and gas. We can hope that this enlightened class will accept that the U.S. must find ways to share equitably with others the limited resources of the planet. As James Speth comments s in his *America the Possible*: "there is no significant relationship between the improvement in happiness and the long-term rate of growth of GDP per capita."[191]

In the context of the desire for change globally, the work *of* Srdja Popovic is particularly relevant. Popovic is the founder of the Centre for Applied Non-Violent Action (CANVAS); he was named by *Foreign Policy* magazine as among the world's top 100 thinkers of 2011. Known internationally for his role in inspiring the Arab Spring protests and for educating activists about non-violent social change in the Middle East, Popovic had first gained stature as a student activist in the ultimately successful campaign to oust President Slobodan Milosevic from power in his native Serbia. To that end, Popovic and his friends mustered 70,000 supporters, enough to persuade 72% of all eligible Serbian voters to vote.[192]

Their future successes hinged on training international activists. They advised start-ups in Georgia, Lebanon, Egypt, Iran, Syria, and the Maldives on how to use inexpensive resources, including DVDs and various other media easily distributed through the internet or by hand, to take on their unjust societies. Popovic even lent his expertise to the Occupy Wall Street movement. He was encouraged by the vigor of this protest as a positive change from the apathy that seems to surround many American concerns, but he cautioned that, in order to be effective, the movement must have a clear goal, a well-thought-out plan to meet that goal, and a desire to spread their message here and abroad.[192]

Popovic paints the issue that triggered Occupy Wall Street as being about much more than the shortcomings of an unregulated capitalism. Rather, he sees it as addressing other major global injustices. He envisions, for example, this same power of small groups of dedicated unaffiliated individuals replacing established political forces and their military component in affecting needed regime changes in oppressive societies.[192]

And so... I would see future movements for change being enabled in our country by a group of educated, experienced youth who see themselves as a force to be reckoned with, a force on at least equal footing with the Wall Street barons and their clients in Washington.

We need look back only 50 years ago to the March on the Pentagon in October 1967 that engaged *100,000 anti-war protesters in helping to* bring an end to the war in Vietnam, or earlier to the 1963 March on Washington for Jobs and Freedom in which Martin Luther King delivered his "I Have a Dream" speech climaxing the successful civil rights movement to see what can be accomplished by groups of our dedicated citizens working together to advance a cause.

By now, you must think that I see the National Service program playing a part in the healing of all our ills. And, you are correct!

Chapter Fourteen
History of Conscription in the US

By the rude bridge that arched the flood, Their flag to April's breeze unfurled, Here once the embattled farmers stood And fired the shot heard round the world.

Ralph Waldo Emmerson — Concord Hymn 1837

You might say… hold on… our conscription practices in the past have worked well for us. Why change things when we've never lost a war? Oh, really? We can hardly call Korea, Vietnam, and Afghanistan resounding "victories." (They could have been, had we not decided each time to "bring a knife to a gun fight.") But that's not really the point. Our history of conscription has probably not been causal in the wars' outcomes. But our methods of assembling a fighting force in time of need have been marked by inconsistencies and inequities.

Early Militias
Let's go back to the 18th century. The colonials relied on civilian militias, raised in each town, to provide local defense. Laws required every able-bodied male to enroll, to be minimally trained,

to be armed, and to serve for limited periods of time in war or emergency, though in some instances individuals were permitted to send a paid substitute. Every year on an appointed date, all business stopped in towns across America for "Training Day," when the men assembled on the town green and locally elected officers would put them through exercises designed to make them ready to fight, if necessary. Then in 1778 the Continental Congress recommended that each of the self-governing states draft men from the various town militias for one year's service. As the ruling was not well-regulated and Congress did not have direct authority to conscript, it failed to fill the ranks of George Washington's Continental Army, now strained to the breaking point with too few recruits. And surely a system that allowed draftees to send paid substitutes was unfair by the standards of any day.

When, during the War of 1812, President James Madison and his Secretary of War James Monroe tried to create a draft to defend the new nation, they were soundly rebuked by antiwar Congressman Daniel Webster of Massachusetts. Daniel Webster's December 9, 1814 address to the House of Representatives contains many of the sentiments of today's anti-draft constituents: "The administration asserts the right to fill the ranks of the regular army by compulsion. Is this, sir, consistent with the character of a free government? Is this civil liberty? Is this the real character of our Constitution? No, sir, indeed it is not....Where is it written in the Constitution, in what article or section is it contained, that you may take children from their parents, and parents from their children, and compel them to fight the battles of any war, in which the folly or the wickedness of government may engage it? Under what concealment has this power lain hidden, which now for the first time comes forth, with a tremendous and baleful aspect, to trample down and destroy the dearest rights of personal liberty?"

Daniel Webster's arguments were, for the time, accepted by Congress, and no draft ensued. But, while the Constitution may not specifically talk about taking "children from their parents and parents from their children, and compel them to fight the battles of any war," Article I, Section 8 does give Congress the power, rather broad at that, to provide for the common Defense and General Welfare of the United States. ... To declare War. ... to raise and support armies ....To provide for calling forth the militia.... [and] To provide for organizing, arming and disciplining the militia."[193]

Civil War Era

It wasn't until the Civil War that the first real military draft was enacted, initially by Confederate President Jefferson Davis' government on April 16, 1862, when the individual states of the Confederacy could not raise sufficient volunteers to defend Secession. A year later, when it became clear that the Union also needed more reinforcements than the individual states could provide, the Enrollment Act of 1863 made conscription an unwelcome necessity for them as well.

Opposition was widespread on both sides.

In the Confederacy, the draft was viewed as a usurpation of individual rights. Under the Confederate Conscription Act, all healthy white men between the ages of 18 and 35 were liable for a three-year term of service. Five months into the draft, the age limit was raised to 45, and as the situation became more desperate the limits were extended to all able-bodied white men between 17 and 50. Exempted were plantation owners and overseers with 20 or more slaves, leading ordinary southern farmers and tradesmen to complain that they were engaged in "a rich man's war, and a poor man's fight."[194] Not surprisingly, compliance with the laws was poor, and Confederate generals were constantly at a loss to find enough conscripts and volunteers fill their ranks.

The draft fared no better in the Union states following the passage of the Enrollment Act. By its terms, each state was assigned a quota to compensate for shortfalls in volunteers, as well as for the high mortalities and desertions. Substitutes were still allowed, and until 1864, men could even avoid service by paying $300 ($4,614 in 2017 dollars) in "commutation" money. Families could save a particular family member, say one who was especially valuable on the farm, from conscription simply by substituting a less valuable family member. But because the North had a far larger population, including immigrants, from which to draw volunteers, and as the volunteers were also offered better pay and signing bonuses, a larger share of the Northern armies continued to be made up of volunteers throughout the war.

Even so, draft dodging, desertion and anti-draft riots were a frequent problem. The Draft Riots of New York City in July 1863 became a major civil insurrection in itself, such that President Lincoln was forced to send several regiments from the Gettysburg battlefield in Pennsylvania to put down the violence. The rioters were overwhelmingly working-class men, primarily ethnic Irish, who felt no particular connection to the plight of enslaved Southern blacks, and competed with freed black men for many of the same low-skilled jobs up north. The rioters also resented the fact that wealthier men could pay their way out of serving either by commutation or substitution. Bribery of enrolling officers was rampant. Conflicts between the practices of state and local governments compounded the problems.

World War I

When the U.S. entered World War I in April 1917, President Woodrow Wilson's administration once more found the nation with a dearth of able-bodied men ready to take up arms. Of the 1,000,000 enlistment target set, only 73,000 volunteered. Conscription once again became the solution. Six weeks after declaring war, the U.S. Congress passed the Selective Service Act, which Wilson signed into law on May 18, 1917. It went a long way toward creating a just and equitable system that the whole nation could accept. The Act read in part:

"That all male persons between the ages of 21 and 30…shall be subject to registration….And any person who shall willfully fail or refuse to present himself for registration or to submit thereto as herein provided shall be guilty of a misdemeanor and shall… be punished by imprisonment for not more than one year."

President Wilson in his Conscription Proclamation, described why such mobilization was needed: "The Power against which we are arrayed has sought to impose its will upon the world by force….There are no armies in this struggle, there are entire nations armed. Thus…it is not an army that we must shape and train for war — it is a Nation….

"The whole Nation must be a team, in which each man shall play the part for which he is best fitted. To this end, Congress has provided that the Nation shall be organized for war by selection; that each man shall be classified for service in the place to which it shall best serve the general good to call him.

"The significance of this cannot be overstated. It is a new thing in our history and a landmark in our progress. It is a new manner of accepting and vitalizing our duty to give ourselves with thoughtful devotion to the common purpose of us all.

"It is in no sense a conscription of the unwilling; it is, rather, selection from a Nation which has volunteered in mass. It is no more a choosing of those who shall march with the colors than it is a selection of those who shall serve an equally necessary and devoted purpose in the industries that lie behind the battle line.

"The day here named is the time upon which all shall present themselves for assignment to their tasks … destined to be remembered as one of the most conspicuous moments in our history. It is nothing less than the day upon which the manhood of the country shall step forward in one solid rank in defense of the ideals to which this nation is consecrated.

"It is important to those ideals no less than to the pride of this generation in manifesting its devotion to them, that there be no gaps in the ranks."[195]

The Selective Service Act allowed exemptions for dependency, essential occupations and religious scruples and prohibited all forms of bounties, substitutions, or purchase of exemptions. Administration of the draft was entrusted to civilian boards composed of leading civilians in each community. Religious scruples were limited; exemptions went to those belonging to religious sects specifically opposed to war including the Quaker, Amish, Mennonite, Moravian, Seventh Day Adventist, and Jehovah's Witnesses' faiths.

Others calling themselves conscientious objectors could gain exemption from combat, but had to serve in a non-combatant role such as the medical corps, engineering, or quartermaster corps. Also exempted were men with many dependents, persons engaged in industries vital to the war effort such as agriculture and the manufacture of military supplies, county and state officials, and certain federal employees.

The Selective Service Act was challenged in a series of cases that went to the Supreme Court in December 1917. In a decision handed down the next month, the Court found the law in full compliance with the Constitution and the Thirteenth Amendment — the prohibition against involuntary servitude, in particular. The Court's Majority Opinion found that "the grant to Congress of power to raise and support armies, considered in conjunction with the grants of the powers to declare war, to make rules for the government and regulation of the land and naval forces, and to make laws necessary and proper for executing granted powers, includes the power to compel military service, exercised by the Selective Draft Law of May 18, 1917."[196] The Court also found that the exercise of federal war powers trumped any state militia powers wherever conflicting interests might arise.

Meanwhile, the draft process went relatively smoothly. Other than some undercurrents of opposition to any involvement in foreign wars, and the disproportionate number of African-Americans and others of the poorer classes who were called up, there were few complaints about favoritism, cronyism or draft dodging. Nearly three million men were inducted into service and sent overseas to reinforce the exhausted ranks of European Allies in a remarkably short time, thanks in large part to the government's effort to build popular support for the war.

World War II

The draft ended with the Armistice in November 1918. Demobilization brought the size of the army down to a level barely adequate to defend U.S. borders in peacetime. By 1922, with isolationism gaining strength, Congress authorized the Regular Army to hold at a strength of 12,000 commissioned officers and 125,000 enlisted men. By 1933, as Hitler came to power, and as unrest gathered in other parts of the world, Chief of Staff Douglas MacArthur reported that the active strength of the U.S. Army was dangerously low, ranking only 17th in the world.

As war clouds gathered, the U.S. initially responded by funneling money and equipment to the embattled victims of German and Japanese aggression. The aid, covered under the Lend-Lease Act, became a tool for remaining officially on the sidelines while our friends and allies struggled unsuccessfully to fend off aggression on their own. Little was done to improve military preparedness until Congress passed the 1940 Selective Training and Service Act by wide margins in both houses. It was effectively the first peacetime draft in the history of the United States, though almost every American sensed that the semblance of peace was about to end in Europe and the Pacific and with it, U.S. neutrality.

The new Selective Service Act called for the registration of all men between 21 and 35 with selection for one year's service by a national lottery. Some 20 million young American men were eligible, but as it turned out, half of them were initially rejected, either for health reasons or because of illiteracy. Then after Japan's December 7, 1941 attack on Pearl Harbor, and Roosevelt's Declaration of War the following day, compulsory service was extended for the duration of the war plus six months. Single men aged 18 to 45 became subject to immediate induction; men with dependents followed; any male 46 to 65 was also required to register just in case. The World War II draft ran from 1940 to 1947, during which time more than 11 million men were inducted. As expected, there was opposition to the draft in some quarters, but it was minor.

Korea and the Cold War

A second peacetime draft was implemented with the passage of the Selective Service Act of 1948. This required all men ages 18 to 26 to register; their obligation was to serve up to 21 months of active duty followed by five years of reserve duty service. As there were sufficient men in uniform left over from World War II service, Selective Service was essentially unused, kept on as a contingency plan should another military action require greater manpower. Then in 1950, the Korean War began and within a few months Congress passed the Universal Military Training and Service Act to meets its demands. Liability for induction rose to

18 ½, and active duty service was extended to 24 months. One of the main advantages of imposing the draft apparently was its positive effect on volunteering; it was said that for every man drafted, four more volunteered, presumably in hopes of negotiating a better duty assignment.

Following the Korean War armistice, Congress passed the Reserve Forces Act of 1955, with the aim of improving the National Guard and the national reserve components. Combined reserve and active duty status was now six years. With a need once again to shrink the military forces, attention was focused on who should be allowed a deferment. Students attending four-year colleges, people employed in war industries and other kinds of essential skilled labor, research scientists, farmers, and married men with children were either given a pass or sent to the end of the line.

Vietnam War

In 1955 the French withdrew from their former Asian colony in Indochina following a decisive defeat at Dien Bien Phu by Communist insurgents. Very soon after the U.S became involved, albeit on a small scale, in the civil war that erupted there between the Communist-sympathizing North Vietnamese and the anti-Communist government of the new Republic of [South] Vietnam on either side of the provisional military demarcation line (17th Parallel) drawn between the two factions by the Geneva Accords in 1954.

Initially American participation was limited to training and other support activities for the South Vietnamese, but it gradually heated up until 1965 when, following a North Vietnamese attack on one of our warships in the Gulf of Tonkin, the U.S. began sending ground combat troops to South Vietnam. Over the years of our involvement, of the total of 8,744,000 men who served, from a pool of 27 million eligible, 2,215,000 were drafted. Allegedly, the vast majority who served did so voluntarily rather than risk being drafted into a duty they did not want. As before, most of the remainder of the draft pool were exempted either because of other military-related service, educational deferment, or disqualification due to mental or physical deficiencies, or criminal backgrounds.

Resistance to the draft and to U.S. participation in the Vietnam War ran high from the beginning, and the calls to end our involvement grew louder and louder as casualties soared. As the annual draft requirements rose dramatically to 328,000 in 1966, so did the probability of being sent into combat. In time, the burning of draft cards became such a widespread form of protest that Congress made it a felony. Some young men fled to Canada to avoid the draft; others extended their college education or sought other deferments, exemptions, and disqualifications. Minorities and the poor were the least equipped to beat the system, and thus made up a disproportionate percentage of combatants as has always been the case.

In 1969, within months of Richard Nixon replacing Lyndon Johnson as president, the first of several waves of U.S. troop withdrawals began in response to public anger. A cease-fire and the last troop withdrawal followed in January 1973. The experience for most Americans had been harrowing, and our taste for war definitely tested.

The Gates Commission and the All-Volunteer Force

On March 27, 1969, less than three months after President Nixon was inaugurated, he announced the creation of a 15-member Advisory Commission on an All-Volunteer Armed Force under the chairmanship of Thomas S. Gates, Jr., former Secretary of Defense. The Commission's assignment was to develop a comprehensive plan to eliminate conscription and move toward an all-volunteer armed force. Among the issues to be considered were a broad range of possibilities for increasing the supply of volunteers, including increased pay, better benefits, recruitment incentives, and other practicable measures to make military careers attractive to more young men. Selection standards, social and economic implications, and estimated costs and savings resulting from an all-volunteer force were also on the table. Standby machinery needed to rapidly reactivate the draft in time of a national emergency was another issue to be discussed and reported on.

The resulting Gates Commission Report charted a new course in which military service was professionalized, military pay was raised, and army life on and off base enhanced. A national advertising campaign was launched on TV to get maximum attention and, beginning on July 1, 1973, all-volunteer recruitment for the Armed Services began in earnest.

The end of the draft and the establishment of the All Volunteer Force coincidentally opened the door to the expansion of women's roles in service. Though many women had served in the Army, Navy, Air Corps, and Coast Guard in World War II in auxiliary roles, including nursing staff, clerks, and even pilots ferrying planes and supplies where needed, their presence had been conditional and without retirement benefits. Now they were welcomed into all the services. The Supreme Court even ruled on their behalf in matters of access to equal benefits for the dependents of women personnel.

The new volunteer program seemed at first to be working. Over 180,000 young men and women enlisted in each of fiscal years 1973, 1974, and 1975, exceeding the U.S. Army Recruiting Command's goals. But in subsequent years problems resurfaced. The registration requirement was suspended in April 1975; with it, the quality of volunteers, their economic and racial diversity, and their motivation began to erode significantly.

The difficulties faced by the United States Army Recruiting Command in the latter half of the decade, and the steps needed to overcome them, serve as lessons for today.[197] In 1980 President Jimmy Carter reinstated the requirement that young men born on or after January 1, 1960 register with the Selective Service System. With the Cold War raging, collective defense pacts in the form of NATO and the Warsaw Pact (eight Central and Eastern European countries) were becoming more active. Also adding to the tension at the end of 1979 was the Soviets invasion of Afghanistan, and Iran's seizure of 60 American hostages in our Tehran embassy in response to our providing sanctuary to the pro-Western Shah of Iran. U.S. confidence in our ability to defend ourselves in time of national crisis was at a low point.

The implementation of the registration requirement is checkered. Theoretically, failure to register is a felony punishable by up to five years imprisonment or a $250,000 fine. Access to numerous federal benefits such as student loans, federal and state training programs, and federal jobs, can also be denied. But no one has been prosecuted for non-compliance since 1986. Many young men register late or not at all without consequences. And women are not under any requirements at all to register.

There have been many attempts to reinstate conscription since Carter's time, none of them gaining traction in Congress. The lengthy wars in Iraq and Afghanistan have placed a particularly heavy burden on our professional army, our National Guard, and our volunteers. The active duty periods of some of the military have been extended for as much as an additional two years in order to maintain adequate troop strength. More significantly, a very large number of active service men have been deployed to war zones for three, four, and up to eight or more tours. This over-dependence on a relative few defies all reasonable justification and has resulted in a high rate of temporary and chronic post-traumatic physical and mental stress for combat troops, destroying countless individuals and their families in the process. If we continue to participate in major military campaigns, we must guarantee sufficient manpower. There is no ethical or strategic alternative

Constitutionality of Universal National Service

As you have read earlier, our history and our Constitution provide us with more than enough legal justification to require conscription in this country whenever the need arises. And no less a man than George Washington has said so. Writing to Alexander Hamilton at the close of the American Revolution, Washington declared: "It may be laid down, as a primary position, and the basis of our system, that every citizen who enjoys the protection of a free government, owes not only a proportion of his property, but even of his personal services to the defence of it."[198]

This of course brings me back to the issue at hand: the constitutionality of the National Service program itself. I have no legal background, and anything that I might write about the question after obtaining legal advice from constitutional experts would bore to death all but those who had run out of anything else to read. Suffice to say that the proponents of the National Service program will be challenged by the many and vocal opponents. I will simply trust that the wisdom of this writer and those of you who agree with me will ultimately prevail. Perhaps it will require a constitutional amendment.

By whatever path we take, the National Service program must indeed be "universal." Everyone of eligible age, male or female, married or single, educated or illiterate, poor or wealthy, connected or not, and with sufficient physical and mental capacity to make a contribution, will participate. So will even the most extreme conscientious objectors, who can carry out one of the humanitarian services to fulfill their obligation. Thus, unlike participation in the many voluntary service programs, those on the margins of society and in most need of the training and experience will be included. Only dangerous criminals and very few others would be excluded.

Undoubtedly, there will be civil libertarians, freedom activists, and other persons and organizations that will fight any compulsory service, military or civilian. To them I say, compulsory service exists now. We are all subject to compulsory education to the age of 16 in some states, to 17 or 18 in others. We are all subject to compulsory jury duty — usually brief, but in some cases, Grand Jury and some capital crimes, lasting for weeks and even months. The State of Maryland requires high school students to complete a certain amount of public service before graduation.

Chapter Fifteen
Nations with Existing Universal Programs

Where is the man who owes nothing to the land in which he lives? Whatever that land may be, he owes to it the most precious thing possessed by man, the morality of his actions and the love of virtue.

Jean Jacques Rousseau — French Philosopher 1712-1778

Israel

When we think of a compulsory military service program, Israel's is usually the first to come to mind. Their continual high-alert status, is caused by their location. Israel is surrounded by mortal enemies and their closest neighbor, Palestine, constantly taunts them with rocket attacks and other hostile actions, which makes their service program needs somewhat different from ours. There are, nevertheless, many similarities from which we can learn.

Since 1949, shortly after the State of Israel was founded, all Israeli citizens over the age of 18 have been subject to conscription into the Israel Defense Forces (IDF). The exceptions, for obvious reasons, are Arab citizens. The term of service is typically three years for men and two years for women. Of those subject to conscription, however, only approximately 50 percent end up serving. Others are excused for a variety of reasons including religious study, low motivation (presumably determined by interview and test), pacifism (conscientious objector), incapability, medical conditions, and criminal records. The last three of these would also serve as an exemption in our program.

Understandably the exemptions are a controversial subject in Israel, especially the religious study exemption, for which yeshiva students qualify by merely declaring that they are fully occupied with the study of *Torah*, the books of Jewish scripture. In theory, religious students are supposed to maintain the exemption only for the duration of their studies, but in practice many of them never serve. Female conscripts can become exempt from military service by declaring that they maintain a religious Zionist way of life; however, many of them then volunteer for an alternate national service called *Sherut Leumi*, a service-oriented program in which the volunteers provide teaching, child care, health care, and other community needs. Some men within the religious Zionist sector can also serve in a separate program called *Hesdar*, which combines advanced religious studies with segregated military service.

Other special arrangements — shorter service terms — are sometimes offered to "Outstanding Athletes" so they can compete in the Olympics for Israel, and to "Outstanding Dancers" and "Outstanding Musicians" so they can continue to improve their artistic skills while serving. There is apparently no give and take on this. It is, simply put, pragmatic favoritism. Should we offer special exclusions along these lines, there should be a cost in the form of an extended term of service later.

One Israeli deferment that makes sense for us is allowing conscripts to continue with high school. We would add a caveat that this would be contingent on meeting certain grade standards, something beyond merely maintaining a passing grade, and committing to the National Service program upon graduation.

Israel offers a variety of other deferment possibilities, but we should avoid these at all costs. We are proposing a <u>universal</u> service program where everyone participates and everyone sacrifices.

The Israeli program offers an educational element with some features not too different from the ones we propose. *Atuda*, their Academic Reserve, enlists and trains soldiers with academic backgrounds in professions vital to the military needs — typically engineering, the law and medicine. The *Talpiot* program trains young people with outstanding academic ability in the sciences, physics, and mathematics. Graduates in both programs serve longer terms, have their tuition paid by the military, and are assigned jobs that use their special training to further the IDF and military security. It is a win-win for everyone and one we should seriously consider incorporating in our National Service program.[199]

Switzerland

On September 22, 2013 a large majority of Swiss voters turned down the referendum to repeal mandatory military service. They supported the government's position that ending conscription would put the nation in great peril, and that the Swiss military would cease to fulfill some of the critical tasks for which it is currently responsible. The results of the referendum also confirmed widely-held beliefs in Switzerland that military service is not only a duty, but that it also exposes all who serve to Swiss citizens from all walks of life and to the regional cultures and languages of the various Swiss cantons.[200] Isn't that exactly what we should be looking for in the U.S.?

In Switzerland, all able- bodied male citizens are conscripted when they reach the age of 18. Women may also volunteer. People who are determined unfit are exempted, but pay an additional 3 percent in annual income tax until age 30; in some cases, alternative social service may be available. Actual service generally begins at age 20, with 118 consecutive days of recruit training. From age 21 to 32 the conscript serves as a "frontline" soldier in training for three weeks per year in 8 of the 12 years. Then from age 33 to 42 he reports for two-week training periods every few years. Finally, from age 43 to 50 he has occasional training in home guard activities for a total of 13 days over this entire period. This all adds up to approximately one year of service spread over the 30-year obligation.

Training includes equipment inspection, target practice, and other traditional military exercises. Members keep their rifles and uniforms in their homes to be ready for immediate mobilization, much as our Minutemen did at the time of the American Revolution. In the past, the Swiss military also kept ammunition at home, but this has been discontinued.[201]

"The Swiss armed forces operate on land and in the air, and also along international waters."[202] Professional soldiers make up approximately five percent of the total forces with the remaining 95 percent being conscripts meeting their mandatory military service requirement. "Because of Switzerland's long history of neutrality, the army does not take part in armed conflicts in other countries, but does take part in peacekeeping missions around the world."[202]

Austria

Austria has compulsory military service for all 18-year-old men. In January 2013 a referendum was held to test the public's view on changing Austria's conscript army to a smaller professional force. As in Switzerland, it was soundly rejected, in this case by a 60-40 vote.[203]

In analyzing the support for the existing system, *New York Times* reporter Melissa Eddy said, "The strongest support for the conscription system came from outside of the capital, Vienna. In the country's rural states, memories of soldiers shoveling snow in villages buried by an avalanche or heaving sandbags to protect towns from rising rivers appeared to have influenced voters.

"Austrian opponents of a move to a professional force had also argued that scrapping conscription would rob the country's social services agencies of thousands of conscientious objectors who carry out a variety of low-paying jobs that would otherwise be difficult to fill, including work done by ambulance drivers and caregivers for the elderly."[203]

Doesn't this strike home with us? With the apparent continuing increase in natural and man-made disasters in the U.S., there is an increasing need for readily available work crews to cleanup and start rebuilding.

South Korea

South Korea has a mandatory military service requirement of approximately two years, varying slightly depending on the branch of service, for males ages 20 to 30 years. Considering their belligerent North Korean neighbor, this is an important subject of national concern. They even resist a place for alternate service for conscientious objectors as urged on them by both the United Nations Human rights Committee and Amnesty International.[204]

Mandatory Military Service Elsewhere

In 2010 Sweden abolished their mandatory military service program. However, with growing concerns about Russian aggression and the future of Europe's reliance on the United States military for protection, they announced on March 3, 2017 that they would reintroduce the program in 2018. The initial draft will cover four thousand men and women.

Denmark has a mandatory service requirement, and all males are notified of their obligation at age 18. However the modest defense needs of Denmark are such as to preclude the conscription of everyone who is eligible. The vast majority of those who serve are volunteers with the balance of conscripts chosen by lottery.

Norway has a similar mandatory requirement, extended recently to women as well. However, the needs of Norway are also such that virtually all participants are volunteers, with few conscripts being called up.

Greece currently has universal mandated military service for all males between the ages of 18 and 45, with a service term of one year for the army and nine months for the air force and navy. In their case, most men eligible for conscription do end up serving.

There are, of course, many other nations around the globe requiring compulsory military service, including some in Asia and some in South America. From that standpoint, we will not be unique. However, our program stands out by offering both a military and a civilian element on equal footing.

Chapter Sixteen
Employment Opportunities

*Far and away the best prize that life offers is the
chance to work hard at work worth doing.*

Theodore Roosevelt

Much has been said and written about the difficulties that our
military veterans face when returning to civilian life. Fortunately,
significant progress has been made to ease the transition over the
past few years. Veterans' unemployment is now actually slightly
lower than the national unemployment rate, and for our youngest
veterans, 18-24 year olds it is significantly lower. Discharge support efforts are paying off.

Discharge Support
To improve on the Veterans Administration discharge support,
the military began phasing out its voluntary three-day transition
assistance briefing in 2012 in favor of a more extensive seven-day
40-hour program. The new program , known as Transition Goals
Planning Success, or Transition GPS for short, was mandatory. The
changes, which have been fully implemented since the end of 2013,
are designed to provide better, more practical, more personalized
services to troops leaving the military. Included are lessons in the

proper length and content of their resumes — for example less military jargon and more "business speak," training in how to do online job searches; and training in the interview process so that veterans can do a better job of translating their military skills to recruiters with specific jobs to fill. [205] Courses on personal finances, family adjustment training, and a review of VA benefits and mentorship opportunities follow. Some of this would, of course, reinforce and refresh lessons learned in the early education phase of their National Service tour. Lastly, veterans are offered different focused tracks depending on veterans' interests — one track for college-bound troops, another for veterans going directly into the civilian job market, and a third for those seeking small business start-up instruction. Transition GPS could be the foundation for a similar program directed not only at those leaving the military option of the National Service program, but also to those leaving the civilian service and international humanitarian aid option. Teaching those returning from National Service would be ideally suited to retirees interested in mentoring.

Two examples of programs that aim to transition veterans from military service to productive citizenship are provided by Arch's Acres run by Colin Archipley, a decorated Marine Corps infantry sergeant, in Escondido, California; and Combat Boots to Cowboy Boots at the University of Nebraska College of Technical Agriculture. Both programs not only offer opportunities to returning veterans, but also aim to bring new life to farming in the rural areas from which approximately 45 percent of the military come. Both programs would also be a very good fit for preparing returning National Service corpsmen for discharge.[206]

In 2015 Bank of America introduced a series of on-line training modules, one of which is called "Captaining Your Career", aimed at educating veterans in promoting themselves to the corporate workplace. This program, too, could be adapted to the discharge curriculum of National Service.[207]

Employment Opportunities

While the national unemployment rate in late 2016 had returned to a traditionally normal level of 4.8%, many of those employed were significantly underemployed; other former workers had dropped out altogether because of very poor job prospects in the future. Many of the youngest cohort would be given a far more promising start in their adult lives if they began with our universal National Service program.

Several years ago NBC correspondent and former Army brat Ann Curry contributed a column in the *Wall Street Journal* entitled "Corporate America's Military Opportunity." In it she recalled the post-World War II period, its concern for the employment prospects of so many returning servicemen, and fears that the pre-war Depression state would resurface. As it turned out, however, these veterans, with their desire to work — and in many cases, their leadership skills — had a very positive effect on the economy and they contributed significantly to the following period of extraordinary growth.[208]

Hiring Veterans

After lamenting for years the fact that we send our youth off to war and then reward the survivors with unemployment, prospects are brightening somewhat as the Iraq and Afghan wars wind down. According to the *Wall Street Journal's* manufacturing reporter James R. Hagerty, corporate America is waking up not only to its responsibilities but to the unique talents that many veterans possess as the result of service. Hagerty cited J. P. Morgan Chase and Lockheed Martin as two of the companies that collectively hope to employ 100,000 veterans by the end of the decade.[209] In a parallel effort, the U.S. Chamber of Commerce is holding "Hiring our Heroes" job fairs. To date more than 28,000 veterans and military spouses have obtained jobs through these events held in all 50 states, Puerto Rico, and the District of Columbia.

Companies naturally like to show they are helping veterans, and publicize their interest. Many employers appreciate the clean-cut appearance and courteous attitude of veterans, but many also find veterans have skills that are hard to find elsewhere. It is incumbent on them, of course, to present these skills in a promising light on a resume. For example, when describing experience, heavy equipment operations and maintenance would have a nice ring. Driving a tank would not! And it's not just jobs like these that we typically equate with the military. More than 150,000 men and women are now working in technical jobs in the military.[210]

Judy Bacchus, chief human-resources officer at Kennametal, a Pennsylvania manufacturer of heavy industry tools, claims that veterans are uniquely suited to being factory supervisors. And Mike Sutherlin, chief executive at Jay Global, Inc., a Milwaukee-based maker of mining equipment, also finds vets to be successful, motivated employees.[209]

While it may be premature to deduce from the above the real positive effect that military training has on employability, there would seem to be ample reason for optimism.

Journalist Michael Ellsberg in his thought-provoking *New York Times* article "Will Dropouts Save America?" refers to a National Bureau of Economic research study that found that "nearly all net job creation in America comes from start-up businesses, not small businesses per se."[211] Many of these new enterprises arise from an entrepreneurial spirit rather than from any formal education that the founders received along the way. Ellsberg continues, "Very few start-ups get off the ground without a wide, vibrant network of advisors and mentors, potential customers and clients, quality vendors and valuable talent to employ. You don't learn how to network crouched over a desk studying for multiple-choice exams. You learn it outside the classroom, talking to fellow human beings face to face."[211]

The National Service program tour of duty would present an excellent opportunity to learn the art of networking here and abroad, especially for those who, when their tour is finished, decide to go directly into the workforce without further specialized training. While there is no denying that for many, a college degree is the right path to a life of success and security, a case can certainly be made for the less formally educated entrepreneur who single-mindedly embarks on a chosen path, avoiding a mountain of college debt in the process.

Chapter Seventeen
Real Heroes

A hero is someone who understand the responsibility that comes with his freedom.

Bob Dylan

Many of the problems with our young result from the examples that society holds up to them as role models. Drugged-up actors and musicians, drug-enhanced baseball players and tour bikers, and even some felons wearing professional sports uniforms, get so much play in the media that it's hardly surprising they are seen by many young people as having achieved something of value. Participation in the National Service program will, I fervently hope, replace those role models with parents, siblings, friends, and other men and women who serve their nation willingly.

Some time ago I attended a ceremony in Danbury, Connecticut, honoring a young man, Todd Angel, who served in Afghanistan and was awarded the Silver Star for bravery under fire. The keynote speaker was a hard-working community volunteer, Mary Teicholz. With her permission, I have included below the entire text of her address:

Hero Speech 2012 "Walk of Honor"

By : Mary Teicholz

Hero: A person of distinguished courage or ability, admired for his or her brave deeds and noble qualities.

"I feel that in this day and age, we have lost sight of what a hero truly is. People who can shoot a basket, throw a 95 mph fastball, write music, sing a song or win an election are not heroes; they are people who possess amazing talents or abilities, but most are not heroes. They get paid millions and millions of dollars and we all feed into their wealth, while our soldiers have to purchase their own boots and some of their uniforms.

"Service members also have to pay for their own medals that they have earned defending our way of life. I think something is very wrong here. Over the years, my husband and I have received requests for equipment from soldiers, because items either weren't available or they were subpar. What was a hero again, and how are they being treated?

"The training our military receives is considered the best in the world so why doesn't their training translate into the civilian world? Why don't their certifications carry over? If they can build a bridge, weld a carrier, be a military police officer, just to name a few, why are they made to jump through hoops when they leave the service? They've already been trained! Maybe that would help with the incidence of homelessness in our veteran communities. How about taking care of them like they have been taking care of us all these years! These people are HEROES! Real heroes, not oh look at me I'm so awesome fake heroes.

"A few months ago, my son was heading for training with one of his army buddies and they were in an airport in Texas. There were people who came up and thanked them for their service, but one gentleman — and I use that term loosely — spit in my son's buddy's face. I never asked what became of the man, because as an army mom you learn quickly not to ask too many questions. The disrespect toward our military members is something I don't think I'll ever understand and I definitely won't put u p with it in my presence. These young men and women love our country in a way few of us will ever be able to comprehend. They wear the American flag on their shoulders with astounding pride and wear their uniforms like a second skin.

"I'm vaguely amused by groups who hold up signs saying, 'So and so for peace.' Newsflash: we all want peace! All you have to do is watch a soldier hold h i s infant child before getting on a plane to deploy to know, without a doubt, that they wish for peace. Or hear the cries of the children saying bye Mommy, bye Daddy as the plane begins to taxi. Or see a mother a nd father crumble at the thought of sending their child off to war. Or the most telling sign of a wish for peace is the complete silence on the airfield after the plane takes off. Soldiers and families a re left without words, only their thoughts.

"So, the next time you see a Veteran or a uniformed military member, aka hero, acknowledge him or her. Help out the spouse of a deployed service member. Mow their lawn, rake their leaves, shovel their snow; ask if they have enough oil in the tank for the winter. Sometimes, the military is a little (a lot) slow with paychecks, so groceries may be needed. Make them laugh to take the edge off. It works wonders for their morale, and ultimately gives piece of mind to their service member.

"The main thing is to start asking our government the hard questions. Why is military funding being cut, why don't our soldiers have the equipment they need, how are you going to improve the health care for our veterans and how do we keep them employed when they return home? And why aren't we properly taking care of our veterans after they have given so much of themselves? And why are these questions even necessary? These are the people who are heroes, these are the people we should all be looking up to and admiring, these are the people we should be putting on pedestals and clamoring to be near, these are the people who are humble in their accomplishments, and these are the people who keep us free. They have fought and are fighting for us, so it's time to return the favor. The military has its mission and our civilian mission needs to be protecting our real American heroes and honoring those who gave the ultimate sacrifice while serving our country. And at the end of the day, isn't that the least we can do?"[212]

Mary's justified passion for the recognition and support of our real heroes comes through loud and clear.

This is an appropriate place to end for now my thoughts on the benefits of universal participation in National Service. With it in place we can truly strengthen this great nation and once again provide the leadership at home and abroad that the world so badly needs.

Your sons and daughters enjoy the benefits and opportunities that life in this country gives all of us. In return, let's give them the chance to give back, in a small way, in service to our country and fellow man by promoting universal National Service.

Step forward, America !

THE END

Epilogue

My Service —
My Family's Service

"How's that man doing?"

"Fine."

"He'd better be."

That was an exchange between the base commanding general and the drill instructor standing in front of me during a company inspection at Parris Island in 1957. My name was on my uniform, I had a college degree from Harvard, and the general and DI knew it, unfortunately for me. Much as I tried not to, I stuck out in this scene. Degrees like mine were rather scarce at Parris Island.

In 1957, when I graduated from Harvard, the Marine Corps had two-year enlistments. I served two years plus a short extension, out of harm's way after the end of the Korean War and before Vietnam had really heated up. The closest I got to action was with the 2nd Division stationed at Camp Lejeune, NC when we were sent overseas to put down an uprising in Lebanon. Yes, we had uprisings even then. Half-way across the Atlantic, the furor died down and our convoy turned 90 degrees and headed south for maneuvers in the Caribbean. We called in naval gunfire on a bunch of old beat-up tanks and other military vehicles on the island of Culebra a few miles northeast of Puerto Rico, and in our spare time enjoyed liberty in San Juan.

Other positive aspects of my tour included a six-month deployment in the Mediterranean on an APA Attack Transport, maneuvers along the North African coast with the British Royal Marines, opportunities to enjoy some liberty in Florence, Italy and on the Riviera, and many wonderful days in the company of fellow enlistees from all walks of life who became very close friends. I think particularly of Bob Donnelly from New York City's Upper West Side, whom I mentioned in Chapter Ten. At the time Bob had only a high school degree, but later had an illustrious business career in key positions at Fortune 500 companies.

While I by no means equate my service to the nation with that of men and women who have been deployed in combat zones, I am proud to have served in a small way. And I believe that all of us have a duty to make a similar contribution.

Why was a Harvard graduate at Parris Island instead of at officers' training (Platoon Leaders Class) at Quantico, Virginia? My father was a naval officer in World War II and so I applied for Naval Reserve Officers Training Corps (NROTC) after entering Harvard in the fall of 1953. I was in good physical shape and athletic enough to be in the starting lineup of the freshman hockey team, but when I took my physical exam, they discovered a spinal problem and turned me down, claiming that I might not be able to stand a watch at sea. In my sophomore year, along with some classmates, I applied for Marine Corps Platoon Leaders Class. When my pals received their orders for summer training, my mail-box remained empty. Eventually I was notified that the Department of the Navy had turned up my previous NROTC denial. Once again I was rejected.

With all other options now closed off, I enlisted as a private in the Marine Corps after graduating from Harvard. Fortunately, they didn't seem to care about my affliction and off I went to Parris Island and later to infantry training at Camp Geiger, a satellite of Camp Lejeune. With good performance came yet another shot at officers' school. When I told them about my initial turn down, the reply was to the effect of "Don't worry, we'll take care of that." This time I turned them down, not willing to spend the additional time involved, and finished out my service as an enlisted man at the rank of corporal.

As previously indicated, my father was a naval officer in World War II; he participated in the landing at Iwo Jima. My brother Tim was a Marine Corps officer who did a tour in Vietnam. A first cousin, a Marine Corps private, received the Purple Heart on Iwo Jima. Another first cousin served in peace time in the Marine Corps, and three brothers-in-law served respectively in the Army, Navy and Marine Corps. One of my two step-grand-sons, Robert, did tours as a Marine infantry corporal in both Iraq and Afghanistan. The other, Matthew, is a West Point graduate, and, as an Army Captain was last deployed in the Sinai Peninsula after a tour of duty in Afghanistan. I am very proud of all of them.

On the other hand, other members of my family have found their calling for service elsewhere, and I am equally proud of their choices. Son Ted, after enjoying the fruits of a very successful career in the financial world now spends a good portion of his time "giving back" by operating and supervising HOMH (Help Our Military Heroes), a 501(c)(3) charity that was started by his wife Laurie and her friend Mary Beth Vandergrift. HOMH raises funds to purchase motor vans to be specially outfitted to accommodate amputees returning from the Iraq and Afghanistan wars. Our other two children, Katie and Chris, are also heavily involved in community service, and my wife Barbara has been a shining example to our children with her many years of voluntary service to Hospice, United Way, her church, and our local library. We, like many of our friends and many of you readers, take seriously the connection between being a good citizen and shouldering public responsibility.

Ted Hollander

Sherman, CT

Acknowledgments

First and foremost I heap thanks on my wife Barbara, who put up with my lack of attention to anything else during the many, albeit short, spurts of activity that I devoted to this project over the many too many months that it took me to complete it. I also wish to thank the rest of my family, as well as the few friends that I let in on this "secret project," all of whom gave me encouragement. My dear friend Bob Fornshell, a decorated World War II veteran, who was the first proof reader of an early manuscript, was particularly encouraging. And last but not least, I offer sincere thanks to my editor Wendy Murphy. I had originally intended to write a paper for my family and possibly local newspapers, but when I decided to proceed into book format, I realized that I would need an editor. The only one I knew of was Wendy, whom I had met briefly at a cocktail party given by mutual friends two or three years ago. She has been of invaluable help, not only with the technical aspects, but also with rearranging my work for better flow, rewording many of my phrases for better clarity, and with some new research and insight on some of the issues.

Bibliography

1   Editorial *Boston Globe* Editorial March 1, 2014

2   Elizabeth Gehrman, "mind the gap", *The Boston Globe Magazine*, Ocrober 2, 2016

3   Professor Daniel N. Robinson, *The Great Ideas of Philosophy*, (Virginia: The Great Courses, 2004), 92

4   Thomas L. Friedman and Michael Mandelbaum, *THAT USED TO BE US: HOW AMERICAFELL BEHIND IN THE WORLD IT INVENTED AND HOW WE CAN COME BACK* (New York: Picador/Farrar, Straus and Giroux, 2011), 296-297

5   Ibid., *309-310*

6   Bob Herbert, "The Way we Treat our Troops", *New York Times*, October 23, 2010

7   R. Russel Rumbaugh, "A Tax to Pay for the War", *New York Times*, February 11, 2013

8   David Leonhardt, "Why Taxes aren't as High as they Seem", *New York Times*, January 20, 2012

9   Bryce Covert, " 'Free Stuff' for Everyone", *New York Times*, October 9, 2015

10 Tom Brokaw, "The Wars that America Forgot About" , *New York Times*, October 18, 2010

11 Thomas E. Ricks, "Let's Draft our Kids", *New York Times*, July 10, 2012

12   Sheen S. Levine and David Stark, "Diversity Makes You Brighter", *New York Times,December 9, 2015*

13   letters to the editor, *New York Times* Feb. 19, 2012

14   David Brooks, "The Great Divorce",*New York Times* Jan. 31, 2012

15   David Brooks, "Time For a Realignment", *New York Times,* September 9, 2016

16   Nicholas Kristof, "U.S.A., Land of Limitations?", *New York Times, August 9, 2015*

17   Joseph Epstein, "How I Learned to Love the Draft", *The Atlantic,* January/February 2015

18   Karl Marlantes, "The War That Killed Trust", *New York Times,* January 8, 2017

19   Stanley McChrystal, "Lincoln's Call to Service and Ours", *Wall Street Journal,* May 30, 2013

20   Charles Swindoll, specific source and date unknown

11   Thomas E. Ricks, "Let's Draft our Kids", *New York Times,* July 10, 2012

21   William F. Buckley, *Gratitude* (New York: Random House, 1990), xviii, 22, 116, 136

22   James M. Stone, *5 Easy Theses,* (New York: Houghton Mifflin Harcourt, 2016), 99, 123-132

23   "Hillary Clinton Announces New National Service Reserve, A New Way for Young Americans to Come Together and Serve Their Communities"
       https://www.hillaryclinton.com/briefing/
       update/2016/09/30

24   David Brooks, "What republicans Should Say", *New York Times,* January 29, 2016

25   Christopher B. Kuch, PhD, "A Call to Arms: Proactively Peotecting the Homeland", *National Guard,*http://www.veteranstoday.com/2016/02/01

26   Chris Jones, "Emanuel on 'Hamilton', Rauner and need for national service", *Chicago Tribune,* August 5, 2016

27 Congressman John B. Larson press release :Larson, Lewis: 'Serve Your Country, Get Relief From Student Debt'" July 14, 2016

28 Mike Tharp, "Your Life - A Converstion with Sebastian Junger", AARP Bulletin, November 2016

29 Michael Gerson, "National service can heal a divided nation", *The Washington Post, June 24, 2013*

30 President Barack Obama, "Presidential Memorandum - Expanding National Service", https://www.whitehouse.gov/the-press-office/2013/07/15

31 Victor R. Martinez, "Most Texas kids physically unfit for military". *El Paso Times*, May 23, 2016

32 Charles Murray, "Narrowing the New Class Divide", *New York Times*, March 8, 2012

33 Michael S. Schmidt, "2 Generals Say Women Should Register for Draft", *New York Times*, February 3, 2016

34 Katie Rogers, "Army Captain to Become First Female Officer Trained to Lead Troops in Combat", *New York Times*, April 29, 2016

35 attributed to Alexander Tytler, Scottish history professor, University of Edinburgh 1887

36 Patricia Cohen, *New York Times* Oct. 17, 2010

37 James Gustav Speth, *America the Possible* (New Haven: Yale university Press, 2012), 111

38 Ibid., 118

39 Nicholas Kristof, "So Little To Ask For: A Home, *New York Times,* April2, 2016

40 Elizabeth Warren, "One Way to Rebuild Our Institutions, *New York Times,* January 29, 2016

41 Kurt Andersen, "The Downside of Liberty", *New York Times*, July 4, 2012

42 Charles Blow, "American Shame", *New York Times,*February 19, 2011

43 Speth, *America the Possible,* 1-2

44   James Fallows, "The Tragedy of the American Military", *The Atlantic*, January/February 2015

45   Thomas Friedman, "Does Obama Have This Right?", *New York Times*, March 23, 2016

46   Andrew J. Bacevich, *Washington Rules: America's path to permanent War*, (Henry Holt and Co., LLC, 2011)

47   Ron Paul - Republican primary debate 2007

48   Congressman Jim Himes, "A note from Congressman Jim Himes - Negotiation is not weakness", March 15, 2016

49   Thomas L. Friedman, "Pass the Books. Hold the Oil", *New York Times*, March 11, 2012

50   David Brooks, "The Temptation of Hillary", *New York Times*, March 6, 2015

51   Jason Dean, "Weak Schools Said to Imperil Security", *Wall Street Journal* Mar. 21, 2012

52   Amanda Ripley, What the U.S. Can Learn From Other Nations' Schools", *New York Times*, December 8, 2016

53   Eduardo Porter, "America's Students Are Lagging. Maybe It's Not the Schools.", *New York Times*, November 4, 2015

54   (www.cfr.org/united-states/us-education-reform-national security/p27618

55   Friedman and Mandelbaum, *THAT USED TO BE US*, 18-19

56   Ibid., 36-37

57   Ibid., 88

58   Speth, *America the possible*, 105

59   Friedman and Mandelbaum, *THAT USED TO BE US*, 235

60   Ibid., 339

61   Claire Cain Miller, "Theme in Obama Farewell: Automation Can Divide Us", *New York Times*, January 16, 2017

62   Andrew M. Cuomo, "Fast-Food Workers Deserve a Pay Raise", *New York Times*, May 7, 2015

63   "How Washington, D.C. Schools Cheat their Students Twice", *Wall Street Journal*, December 1, 2012

64   Edward P. Lazear and Simon Janssen, "German Offers a Promising Jobs Model", *Wall Street Journal"*, September 9, 2016

65   Jeffrey J. Selingo, "College Isn't Always the Answer", *Wall Street Journal*, May 27, 2016

66   Mark Schneider, "A Bachelor's Defree Isn't the Only Path to Good pay", *Wall Street Journal*, June 4, 2015

67   Thomas L. Friedman, "Come the Revolution", *New York Times*, May 16, 2012

68   Gregg Easterbrook, "When Did Optimism Become Uncool?", *New York Times*, May 15, 2016

69   Andrew Ross Sorkin, "The Obama Recovery", *New York Times Magazine*, May 1, 2016

70   Michael Grabell, *Money Well Spent?*, (New York: Public Affairs, 2012) 138

71   Thomas L. Friedman "Capitalism, Version 2012", *New York Times*, March 14, 2012

72   Bjorn Lomborg, "Trade-Offs for Global Do-Gooders", *Wall Street Journal*, September 19-20, 2015

73   General H. Norman Schwarzkopf with Peter Petre, *It Doesn't Take a Hero,*(New York: Bantam Books, 1993) 585

74   Speth, *America the Possible,*40-41

75   David Gergen "Plus, 5 Reasons To Stay Positive", *Parade*, November 4, 2012

76   Thomas L. Friedman, "Who Are We", *New York Times*, February 17, 2016

77   David Brooks, "Is U.S. as Great as U.S. Athletes Are?", *New York Times*, August 19, 2016

78   Emily Badger, "Actually, Many of America's 'Inner Cities' Are Doing great", *New York Times*, October 12, 2016

11   Thomas E. Ricks, "Let's Draft our Kids", *New York Times*, July 10, 2012

79   William F. Buckley, *Gratitude*, (New York: Random House, 1990), 125

80   James M. Stone, *5 Easy Theses*, (New York: Houghton Mifflin Harcourt, 2016), 130

81   Matthew R. Costlow, "A Bad Time to Cut U.S. Nuclear capability, *Wall Street Journal,* March 25, 2016

82   Peter Bergen, "Can We Stop Homegrown Terrorists?", *Wall Street Journal,* January 23-24, 2016

83   David Brooks, "How Radicals Are Made", *New York Times,* December 8, 2015

84   William J. Byron, "How to make America great again? National service", *Danbury News-Times,* November 30, 2015

85   Friedman and Mandelbaum, *THAT USED TO BE US,* 350-351

86   Thomas L. Friedman, "Win, Lose, But No Compromise", *New York Times,* August 31, 2016

87   Ross Douthat, "Bloomberg, LaPierre and the Void", *New York Times,* December 23, 2012

88   David Brooks, "Bold on Both Ends", *New York Times,* April 12, 2013

89   Thomas L. Friedman, "Help Wanted: Leadership", *New York Times,* September 25, 2011

90   "Republican Budget Tantrum", *New York Times,* February 10, 2016

91   Steven Rattner, "Foiling Obama, Congress Made Trump", *New York Times,* April 13, 2016

92   "The Senate's Confrirmation Shutdown", *New York Times,* June 9, 2016

93   "The Benghazi Committee's Final Act", *New York Times,* June 4, 2016

94   Stephen R. Weissman, "Congress and War - How the House and the Senate can Reclaim Their Role", *Foreign Affairs,* January/February 2017

95   Philip K. Howard, "The Crippling Hold of Old Law", *Wall Street Journal,* April 2-3, 2016

96   E. J. Dionne, "Celebrating the nation that can't stay still", *Danbury News-Times,* July 5, 2016

97 Friedman and Mandelbaum, *THAT USED TO BE US,* 352

98 Irwin Shishko, Letter to the Editor, *Wall Street Journal,* September 29, 2016

99 House SpeakerPaul Ryan, "The State of American Politics", http://www.speaker.gov/press-release/full-text-speaker-ryan, March 23, 2016

101 Philip J. Cook and Kristin A. Goss, *The Gun Debate,* (New York: Oxford University Press, 2014) 135

100 Stephan Lesher, "A Cacaphony of Cowardice", *Danbury News-Times,* July 5, 2015

102 Kevin Quealy and Margot Sanger-Katz, "The U.S. Is a World Apart In Gun Death Rates", *New York Times,* June 14, 2016

103 Nicholas Kristof, "Some Inconvenient Gun Facts for Liberals", *New York Times,* January 17, 2016

104 Cook and Goss, *The Gun Debate,* 143

105 "Gun-Control Groups Push Growing EvidenceThat Laws Lead to Less Violence", *New York Times,* October 12, 2016

106 Cook and Goss, *The Gun Debate,* 34

107 Charles M. Blow, "Focus on Illegal Guns", *New York Times,* January 11, 2016

108 "The Republican Fear of Facts on Guns", *New York Times,* December 24, 2015

109 Cook and Goss, *The Gun Debate*

110 Frederick W. Smith, "How Trade Made America Great", *Wall Street Journal,* March 26-27, 2016

111 Jared Bernstein, "Free Trade Is Fading. Now What?", *New York Times,* March 14, 2016

112 Thomas L. Friedman, "At Lunch, Trump Give Critics Hope", *New York Times,* November 23, 2016

113 Eduardo Porter, "Government: The Real Job Creator", *New York Times,* May 11, 2016

114 David M. Herszenhorn, "It's a Stretch, but McConnell Is Reaching Across the Aisle", *New York Times,* April 25, 2016

115   Curtis Bradley and Jack Goldsmith, "Don't Let Americans Sue Saudi America", *New York Times.* April 22, 2016

116   Frank Bruni, "Obama's Gorgeous Goodbye", *New York Times,* May 11, 2016

117   Alan S. Blinder, "A Glimpse of What Bipartisan Compromise Looks like". *Wall Street Journal,* December 31, 2015

118   David Brooks, "New Life in The Center", *New York Times,* November 29, 2016

119   Thomas L. Friedman, "Dump G.O.P. For a Grand New Party", *New York Times,* June 8, 2016

120   Arthur C. Brooks, "Bipartisanship Isn't for Wimps, After All", *New York Times,* April 30, 2016

121   Charles M. Blow, "Learning Lessons From Outrage", *New York Times,* March 21, 2016

122   *The Declaration of Independence*

123   *The Constitution of the Unites States of America*

124   *Bill of Rights*

125   *Amendments XIII, XV, and XIX to The Constitution of the United States of America*

126   George W. Bush and Karen Hughes, *A Charge to Keep* (Harper Collins, 1999) 240

127   http://abcnews.go.com/Politics/story?id=123290)

128   First Bush-Kerry debate Miami FL Sept. 30, 2004

129   George W. Bush address to the U N General Assembly Sept. 21, 2004

130   Adam Smith *Wealth of Nations*

131   George W. Bush State of the Union address Jan. 31, 2006

132   *Dana Milbank, Washington Post* Dec. 21, 2003

133   "Jobs for the Young in Poor Neighborhoods", *New York Times,* March 14, 2016

134   Nicholas Kristof, "When Whites Just Don't Get It, Revisited", *New York Times,* April3, 2016

135   Deborah M. Seymour, Letter to the Editor, *New York Times,* July 4, 2016

136 Tamar Lewin, "Obama Wades into Issue of Raising Dropout Age", *New York Times,* January 26, 2012

137 Henry M. Levin and Cecelia E. Rouse "The True Cost of High School Dropouts", *New York Times,* January 26, 2012

138 Charles M. Blow, "These Children are Our Future", *New York Times,* June 15, 2013

139 Elizabeth Kolbert, "Spoiled Rotten-Why do Kids Rule the Roost?", *New Yorker,* July 2, 2012 -

140 Alexis de Tocqueville, *Democracy in America*"On Association", Chapter 5, Part II

141 Speth, *America the Possible,* 31

142 David Brooks, "The Fragmented Society", *New York Times,* May 20, 2016

143 "Being American in the Trump Years", *New York Times,* November 10, 2016

144 Bob Greene, "The Military-Free 2016 Contenders", *Wall Street Journal,* March 15, 2016

145 Joe Nocera, "Reading, Math and Grit"/"A Ray of Hope in Education", *New York Times,* September 8, 2012

146 Friedman and Mandelbaum, *THAT USED TO BE US,* 376

147 Elizabeth A. Harris, "One Lesson: Judge Judy Isn't on the Supreme Court", *New York Times,* November 10, 2016

148 Eileen Fitzgerald, "We must have younger people civically engaged", *The News Times* Danbury, CT, October 10, 2013, A2

149 Barack Obama at a Democratic National Committee fundraiser in Atherton, California April 4, 2013

150 Nina Sovich, "Econ 101 After recess", *Wall Street Journal",* March 2, 2016

151 Adam Smith, *Wealth of Nations*

152 Donald Marron, *30 - Second Economics,* (Ivy Press, 2010) 136

153 Stephen Moore, "The Man who Saved Capitalism", *Wall Street Journal,* July 31, 2012

154 Marron, *30-Second Economics,* 17

155   *Ibid., 51*

156   "The Center for Financial Literacy", http:/www.champlain. edu/centers-of-excellence/center-for-financial-literacy

157   John Pelletier *National Report Card on State Efforts to Improve Financial Literacy in High Schools*, (Champlain College, 2013), 2

158   Stephanie Taylor Christensen, "Money 101: That's a course young Americans wish they'd taken in school", *USA Today*, October 6, 2016

159   Neal Gabler, "My Secret Shame", *The Atlantic*, May 2016

160   Friedman and Mandelbaum, *THAT USED TO BE US*, 301

161   Timothy Egan, "The Dumbed Down Democracy", *New York Times*, August 27, 2016

162   Friedman and Mandelbaum, *THAT USED TO BE US*, 156-157

163   Ibid., 160

164   Ibid., 161

165   Thomas Shanker,"Djibouti Outpost Behind Somalia Rescue Is Part Of New Defense Strategy", *New York Times* Jan. 26, 2012

166   Jeffrey Sachs Keynote Address to the Development Policy Forum in Berlin in 2002

167   Salil Shetty, Director, United Nations Millenium Campaign, http://www.civicus.otg/content/e-CIVICUS444-aid_and_ global_economic_crisis.html

168   James Dao, "Ad Campaign for Marines Cites Chaos as a Job Perk", *New York Times*, March 10, 2012

169   Dillon Banerjee, *The Insider's Guide to the Peace Corps* (Berkeley: Ten Speed Press, 2009) 8

170   Ibid., 38

171   Ibid., 41

172   Ibid., 43

173   Friedman and Mandelbaum *THAT USED TO BE US*, 311

174   James Bovard, "The Reality of Feel-Good Government", *Wall Street Journal*, June 13, 2013

175   Dion Nissenbaum, "Roads to Nowhere: U.S. Program to Win Over Afghans Fails", *Wall Street Journal*, February 10, 2012

176   Teach For America "Welcoming Teach For America's 2016 Corps!"
       https://www.teachforamerica.org/Top-stories/Welcoming-teach-americas-2016-corps

177   Nicholas Kristof, "A Millennial Named Bush", *New York Times*. July 26, 2015

178   "Missionaries Around the World", http://www.mormon.org/values/missionary-work, copyright holder Intellectual Reserve, Inc.

179   Laurie Goodstein, "More Mormon Women Enroll as Missionaries", *New York Times*, November 3, 2012

180   James Faulconer, "Mormon Missionaries", http://www.patheos.com//Mormon/Mormon-Missionaries-James-Faulconer-01-24-2013.html

181   Nicholas D. Kristoff, "After Recess: Change the World", *New York Times*, February 5, 2012

182   Steve Phillips, "How to Build a Democratic Majority", *New York Times*, October 5, 2016

183   Ralph Nader, *Breaking Through Power*, (San Francisco: City Light Publishers, 2016) 132-137

184   Thomas L. Friedman, "Sorry, Kids. We Ate It All.", *New York Times*, October 16, 2013

185   Charles M. Blow, "The Young Are the Restless", *New York Times*, April 6, 2013

186   Speth, *America the Possible*, 21

187   Ibid., 6

188   Ibid., 138

189   Ibid., 133

190   "The Road to the New Economy", www.bcorporation.net/what-are-b-corps/the-non-profit-behind-b-corps

191   Speth, *America the Possible,* 82

192   Liel Leibovitz, "The Revolutionist", *The Atlantic,*Mar. 2012

193   Daniel Webster (December 9, 1814 House of Representatives Address)

194   Wikipedia contributors, "Conscription in the United States ", *Wikipedia, The Free Encyclopedia,*
http://en.wikipedia.org/w/index.php?title=Conscription_in_the_United_States&oldid=623929048 (accessed September11, 2014)

195   President Woodrow Wilson on the Selective Service Act of 1917

196   *United States Constitution, Art.* I, § 8

197   Thomas W. Evans, *Army History, The Professiona Bulletin of Army History,* #27 (Summer 1993) p. 40

198   "Sentiments on a Peace Establishment" in a letter to Alexander Hamilton (2 May 1783) published in *The Writings of George Washington* (1938). Edited by John C. Fitzpatrick, Vol. 26. p.289

199   Wikipedia contributors, "Conscription in Israel", *Wikipedia, The Free Encyclopedia*
http://en.wikipedia.org/w/index.php?title=Conscription_in_Israel&oldid=619827743 (accessed Sept. 11, 2014)

200   Geneva AFP "Swiss government urges voters to keep military conscription"
http://foxnews.com/world/2013/08/16/swiss-government-urges-voters-to-keep-military-conscription

201   Frankly Speaking May 16, 2007 "Swiss Military Service", http://frankcomment.blogspot.com/2007/05/swiss-military-service.html

202   Wikipedia contributors, "Military of Switzerland", *Wikepedia, the Free Encyclopedia,*
http://en.wikipedia.org/w/index.php?title=Military_of_Switzerland&oldid=623573016 (accessed Sept. 11, 2014)

203   Melissa Eddy, "Austrians Appear to Reject Changes to
         Conscript Army", *New York Times*, January 21, 2013

204   Choe-Sang-Hun, "South Korean Jehovah's Witnesses Fight
         Stigma of Not Serving in Army", *New York Times*, October 4,
         2015

205   Benjamin Kesling and Laura Meckle, "Reboot Set for
         Program that Moves Vets to Civilian Life", *Wall Street Journal*,
         July 23, 2012

206   Patricia Leigh Brown, "Helping Soldiers Trade Their Swords
         for Plows", *New York Times*, February 6, 2011

207   Joe Mullich, "Lost in Translation", *Wall Street Journal*,
         November 11, 2015

208   Ann Currry, "Corporate America's Military Opportunity",
         Wall Street Journal, March 27, 2012

209   James R. Hagerty, "Firms Press to Hire Young Veterans", *Wall
         Street Journal*, October 15, 2012

210   Michelle Obama and Jill Biden, "Veterans With Job Skills
         America Needs", *Wall Street Journal*, May 5, 2016

211   Michael Ellsberg, "Will Dropouts Save America", *New York
         Times*, October 23, 2011

212   Speech 2012 at Danbury, CT War Memorial Walk of Honor -
         Mary Teicholz

CPSIA information can be obtained
at www.ICGtesting.com
Printed in the USA
FSOW02n1502110717
36192FS